D0814717

WITH'S GODS GRACE...

Barbara Arbuckle

Contributors: Sister Janice McGrane, SSJ,
Elisa Taylor Berry, Arlene Finocchiaro, Annette Hug

WESTBOW
PRESS®
A DIVISION OF THOMAS NELSON
& ZONDERVAN

Copyright © 2016 Barbara Arbuckle.

All rights reserved. No part of this book may be used or reproduced by any means, graphic, electronic, or mechanical, including photocopying, recording, taping or by any information storage retrieval system without the written permission of the author except in the case of brief quotations embodied in critical articles and reviews.

Scripture texts in this work are taken from the New American Bible, revised edition© 2010, 1991, 1986, 1970 Confraternity of Christian Doctrine, Washington, D.C. and are used by permission of the copyright owner. All Rights Reserved. No part of the New American Bible may be reproduced in any form without permission in writing from the copyright owner.

Scripture quotations marked (NIV) are taken from the Holy Bible, New International Version®, NIV®. Copyright © 1973, 1978, 1984, 2011 by Biblica, Inc.™ Used by permission of Zondervan. All rights reserved worldwide. www.zondervan.com The "NIV" and "New International Version" are trademarks registered in the United States Patent and Trademark Office by Biblica, Inc.™

This book is a work of non-fiction. Unless otherwise noted, the author and the publisher make no explicit guarantees as to the accuracy of the information contained in this book and in some cases, names of people and places have been altered to protect their privacy.

WestBow Press books may be ordered through booksellers or by contacting:

WestBow Press
A Division of Thomas Nelson & Zondervan
1663 Liberty Drive
Bloomington, IN 47403
www.westbowpress.com
1 (866) 928-1240

Because of the dynamic nature of the Internet, any web addresses or links contained in this book may have changed since publication and may no longer be valid. The views expressed in this work are solely those of the author and do not necessarily reflect the views of the publisher, and the publisher hereby disclaims any responsibility for them.

Any people depicted in stock imagery provided by Thinkstock are models, and such images are being used for illustrative purposes only. Certain stock imagery © Thinkstock.

ISBN: 978-1-5127-4458-3 (sc)
ISBN: 978-1-5127-4460-6 (hc)
ISBN: 978-1-5127-4459-0 (e)

Library of Congress Control Number: 2016909009

Print information available on the last page.

WestBow Press rev. date: 06/30/2016

I will praise you, Lord, with all my heart; I
will declare all your wondrous deeds.
(Psalm 9:2)

Her life was given to Jesus.
Her sufferings were tied to Jesus.
Her connections brought us to Jesus.
Her writings told of Jesus.
Her work for the unloved and disabled were for Jesus.
Her weakened state reached for Jesus.
Her prayer was to be with Jesus.

Thank you Jesus for taking our beloved friend to Heaven.

Sister Janice McGrane, SSJ passed on Monday, June 27, 2016.

ACKNOWLEDGEMENTS

Barbara Arbuckle

*T*he seed was planted in my heart to write about God's grace nearly ten years ago. It has been a journey of faith among all five authors.

I would like to thank my best friend and greatest love here on earth, my husband, Jim. I thank my children, James and Julie, her husband David, my grandsons Colin, Ian and Owen for their love and support. I thank my mother for sharing and encouraging my love for Jesus and Mary.

I am forever grateful to Sister Janice McGrane, Elisa Taylor Berry, Arlene Finocchiaro and Annette Hug. This book is their faith story as well as my own. We all have taken a deep look into our lives and come out stronger and more in love with our Lord.

I especially thank Arlene and her husband, Ray Finocchiaro, for their countless hours of editing. We would not have been able to put this together without their guidance and support.

I am so blessed to have had the hours with Monsignor Ralph J. Chieffo of Saint Mary Magdalen Parish in Media, PA. He read our writings, shared his thoughts, guided us and believed that our book would be an inspiration to help others. He prayed over me and was a great source of inspiration to me as I then encouraged us all to look to sacred scripture and the fruits of the Holy Spirit.

I give thanks to Kathy Hack for her help in driving Sister Janice from Oreland to West Chester and a return trip so she could be with us as a group.

CONTENTS

Introduction (Barbara Arbuckle)..xi

Chapter 1:   Surrender Your Soul (Barbara Arbuckle).....................1

Chapter 2:   Become Like a Child (Barbara Arbuckle)..................13

Meeting Elisa (Barbara Arbuckle)..25

Chapter 3:   Follow the Grace (Elisa Taylor Berry)......................26

Chapter 4:   It All Began with Love (Elisa Taylor Berry)..............37

Meeting Arlene (Barbara Arbuckle)...50

Chapter 5:   Expect the Unexpected (Arlene Finocchiaro).............51

Chapter 6:   Walk into the Light (Arlene Finocchiaro)................65

Meeting Sister Janice (Barbara Arbuckle)................................80

Chapter 7:   Grace: God's Communication Lourdes, 1988
             (Janice McGrane, SSJ)...81

Meeting Annette (Barbara Arbuckle).......................................91

Chapter 8:   Childhood Innocence (Annette Hug)......................92

Chapter 9:   Mercy Upon Mercy (Annette Hug)........................101

Epilogue (Barbara Arbuckle)..115

References..117

About the Authors...119

INTRODUCTION

There is only one reason for this book and that is to tell you that God loves you. It is quite simple. He is our Father and we are his children. He gives us grace to carry us through the dark periods and difficult times.

I promise you I am a simple person. I have faith in God and know that he is my strength. I went through a dark period in my life and prayed hard to come out of it. I did come out of it and that is because God gave me the grace that I needed. We receive whatever it is that is needed when we ask God for help. It is that simple.

This book has unfolded like a tapestry. All five women, including myself, have been brought together for a purpose. We were strangers and yet over the past few years we have become great friends and support one another in our spiritual journey. God is the master weaver and we weave the threads we are given. Tapestries are created by many weavers, each following a plan. Every person has a small portion of the bigger picture, the one God has planned for us to follow. The pattern weaves lives together in a picture that only he can see from the front of the tapestry. We weave little bits and pieces from the back, our day-to-day struggles and joys, seeing the final result only when he shows it to us, his children in heaven. We are all connected by the Great Weaver's plan and each thread is important to the patterns in the tapestry.

I will introduce each woman and then you can step inside their lives. You will grow in faith as you experience along with them how God opened their hearts. Remember the message is always the same and not complicated. It is that God loves you as well as me. He does not pick favorites. He showers you with graces that are needed for you and you alone.

CHAPTER I

SURRENDER YOUR SOUL

"We have a fifty-year-old female on the way," said the paramedic.

He asked me to pick up my arm for the IV but I lay on the stretcher with no strength. I could feel the ambulance pulling away from my house.

I had been home alone, weak and light-headed. I was sweating and trembling. My whole body began to shake and my legs went limp. My heart was beating uncontrollably and it was the only noise I heard.

I called my sister and told her I was calling 911 since I believed I was dying. Starting to fade away, I called my daughter to let her know I was dying—but that I felt it was my time to go and that was okay with me.

I remember the first part of the ambulance ride like it was yesterday. I was far away and very peaceful, watching my body from a distance. I was happy where I was and had no desire to return. Then I knew that my life was changing. I do not know if this was a near-death experience or not but I know that it was complete peace.

The next thing I remember was waking up in the hospital and surrounded by my family. I begged forgiveness, as I never meant to bother anyone. Routine tests concluded that this was my second panic attack.

My first attack occurred as the school year was coming to an end. We had been preparing our classroom for the mothers' tea, and the classroom was full of unfinished projects. My aide came to the classroom so I could go to lunch. I remember sharing stories with my grade partner and another teacher. We were all trying to figure out our busy lives.

The next thing I knew, I was leaving the lunch room holding onto the door. I nearly fell over and walked in a fog to the nurse. She was kind and noticed I was shaking and had a rapid heartbeat. She called 911 and I later woke up in the hospital with my daughter next to me. I was told I had had a panic attack. Tired but recovering, I returned to school and completed the year.

Since I now had two ambulance rides within one month, my family was deeply concerned about me. My family doctor recommended antidepressants and that I see a therapist. I took one pill and let my family know that I knew something was terribly wrong. I did not feel that taking pills was the right answer.

I quickly spiraled into deep depression. It only lasted weeks but was a very dark period of my life. Looking back, I understand how awful depression really is. You are alone, suffering in darkness, and afraid.

This was the darkest period of my life. Days and nights were all combined. I couldn't sleep and was agitated. My mind was confused. I wandered around the house aimlessly and felt another panic attack coming on. I paced the hallway breathing in short breaths. I worried endlessly. The thought of another ambulance ride to the hospital increased my panic.

I didn't eat or go anywhere. When I saw my children sitting at the kitchen table watching me, I told them, "I cannot feed you." They looked lovingly at me and did not want food. All they wanted was my well-being. My husband tried to understand and help in any way he could.

My sister was the angel who came daily to my side. She was peaceful, gentle and filled with compassion. She listened as I began to tell her how hard it was to take care of so many people. I was so busy. I just shut down. I told her how I tried to control every event of my life and how I worried about family, friends, my kindergarten students and anyone else who needed me. I was worn down and the worries of my life had consumed me.

My sister took me to a therapist. In addition to medication, my therapist encouraged me to give my worries over to someone or something. I immediately told her that I would like to give them to Mary, the mother of Jesus. She encouraged me to do so. Her support was a tremendous comfort to me.

I began feeling a little better and kept reading the Psalms from the Bible over and over. I still suffered greatly, feeling so alone and confused. Even after practicing deep breathing, meditation and muscle relaxation, I was still anxious. I worried about another panic attack coming on and how I would ever feel normal again.

My mother told her sister about my depression. My aunt said, "Surrender your soul." I thought this sounded crazy, but I knew that I had a soul and that it was being tortured. I asked God to take my weakness and be my strength. I was completely empty and had no more to give. Surrendering my soul was letting go of myself and what I wanted. It was doing the will of God.

In my weakness, I wanted God to take over for me. I wanted him to be in charge and not me. So I prayed and surrendered my soul. There was not an immediate answer but, deep within, I knew that God was in control and that I would be okay. I began eating and sleeping. I started reading about depression and anxiety. I was careful to eat better and to exercise. Little by little, my life changed. I was stronger and clearer in my thinking. I felt so thankful to God.

God's healing grace changed my life. I wanted to thank God by telling others. I knew depression and I knew it deeply within my soul.

It was despair and ugly. It was a place you never want to go. I feel such compassion for people who suffer with depression because they are in a very dark place. People have so many reasons for despair, but God can bring you out of this dark place.

I slowly recovered by the grace of God. I believe he heard my plea for help and answered it. Regaining my strength and a purpose to get up each day, I saw blessings all around me. Treasuring my family, I wanted so much to hug them and let them know that God was my strength. I will tell you the same words come from my mouth close to fifteen years following this event: the Lord is my strength.

Blessed be the Lord, who has heard the sound of my pleading.
The Lord is my strength and my shield,
in whom my heart trusts.
I am helped, o my heart rejoices; with song I praise him.
(Psalm 28: 6–7)

Working to care for myself, I followed recommendations for proper nutrition and exercise. I realized there was no quick and easy fix to what troubles us in life. But I did know that God loves us and is waiting for us to simply ask for his help. It comes and sometimes it is through other people, such as a caring neighbor or a loving relative. Or sometimes it comes by just being quiet and knowing that an all-powerful and loving God is there for you.

Returning to school in the fall, I told the many curious people who witnessed me being taken away in my first ambulance ride that I was fine and that God's grace had carried me through it all. I taught kindergarten for another six years and I did so with a great love for the children and a desire to share the love that God gave me.

With this healing event in my life, I understood that I had been emotionally unwell and living in darkness. I also understood that I was now changed. New strength came from giving myself completely to God and the intercession of Mary.

People who love the Blessed Mother will tell you that she always points you to her son, Jesus. I began reading the Bible with a great thirst and I would often attend Bible studies. I will never stop learning from Jesus, my teacher. I believe he hears me and wants me to trust in him. I do trust him and talk to him as my friend.

I am not a theologian or spiritual leader. I am a simple person with my own struggles and heartaches. I want to share that grace is a gift from God—and it is real.

After sixteen years of teaching full-day kindergarten, I retired and began to care for my mother. She was in her eighties and couldn't keep up with her home. My husband graciously agreed to our caregiving. I knew that I had to ask God for the grace to be patient and kind. I recall telling a priest that this was a concern for me. He told me, "Remember that the grace is always there, but you must simply ask." I did and still do.

I left my empty classroom on the first day of my retirement and carried a picture of Jesus. It was given to me by a religious sister years ago. The picture was large, approximately two feet high. I used to keep it over my desk and looked at it often to remind me to treat the children as Jesus would. I walked out of the classroom telling my aide that I was leaving with Jesus. I walked away from one part of my life and walked into a new role as caregiver. I needed to carry Jesus along with me.

"Surrender your soul" took on new meaning in my life. It is the desire to let God be in charge. It is to surrender daily to his will. It is to trust in him. How often are we called to take on new unexpected roles? We cannot always choose our path and surrendering to God's plan is the only way through.

**My grace is sufficient for you, for power
is made perfect in weakness.
(2 Corinthians 12:9)**

My mother was slowly moving her belongings into my home. One evening she came holding a statue of Mary carefully in her arms and told me, "I am here now." We both relied on Jesus and Mary, and we prayed every day to both of them for the next seven years that she lived with us.

My surrender to God's plan for caring for my mother was also my mother's surrender—a surrender to the move, changes in friends, and loss of independence and physical abilities. His plan also opened new opportunities to learn and love for the both of us.

Being a caregiver is not easy. Getting old is not easy. I watched my mom lose almost every person she knew, lose her hearing and most of her eyesight, have aches and pains, get confused, experience depression and worry until she was completely exhausted.

In the beginning years of caregiving, she accompanied me one day a week to serve food to the homeless at the St. Agnes Day Room. There you saw the face of Jesus among others. It was through kind and loving words. It was in giving smiles and hugs. It was in the prayers that were said. These were warm experiences my mother and I were able to share together.

With her failing eyesight, my mother needed other fulfilling experiences directed to her level of care. She began attending a senior center two days a week for five years. It was there that she met an angel. You may question why I say an angel but, when you meet one, you know it. When you enter a new environment at any age, you feel uncertain. A woman at the center came and sat across from my mother at the coffee table. She showered her with smiles and an outreached hand. Tears welled in my mother's eyes. Since she was afraid to meet new people, she wondered what was going to happen. I realize now that many of my kindergarten students felt the same way.

When you are in your eighties, you feel the same feelings. The woman showing kindness became my mother's friend for the next five years. What stood out most was the way she welcomed others with such love and compassion. It was never about her, but only about you, and what she could do for you. My mother was touched deeply that her friend was so sensitive to a woman who was sick and all alone. She kissed her on her bald head, took her hand and found her a seat. She knew this woman was in need of the extra help. I can make similar comparisons to the young children that I taught. Maybe the young as well as the old can remind us of how much we need each other.

When my mother was ninety, she lacked the independence needed to continue at the senior center. So I hired a woman to come into my home. She happened to be a Gospel singer. She told my mother that when you worry, you stress. When you stress, you become sick. She asked if she could sing for us. We could not believe what came out of her mouth. The words were not to worry, place your trust in him, and give it to the Lord. Honestly, her voice was as if Whitney Houston was in our home. I cried and got the chills. It felt like we were receiving a singing telegram from God himself.

As a caregiver, I kept in mind to treat my mother as I would want to be treated. I certainly hope that someone will be kind to me as I age. Certainly we will all suffer. This is part of life. My mother would tell her brother about her aches and pains and he would remind her of all the suffering of Jesus. We can join our suffering to Jesus and we know that he will be with us. He understands.

When we look at our sufferings, they are quite small in comparison to many others. We all are joined in pain of one kind or another. Jesus' resurrection gives us the hope and light that dispels all our darkness.

When my mother turned ninety, her health began to fail. I had noticed the slow process of increasing aches and pains. We certainly had more than our share of giggles to ease the pain. She and I began each morning with medication, eye drops, hearing aids, putting on glasses, and teeth. Getting dressed was a challenge since standing independently was hard. I pulled out a couple of prayers, and then we began our day. I understand why it seems a lot easier to just stay in bed. But the movement is essential in keeping the body going. How many times did I hear, "Either move it or lose it?"

My mother had been very active with children, grandchildren and an active husband. But slowly life changed. She was a golfer, member of a bowling league, played cards, traveled a lot with my father, and certainly lived a full life. She loved to attend daily Mass and stayed to pray the rosary. Life was good.

When she needed assistance to walk, I did not have the strength to pick her up. Another surrender was in store for both of us. Even with the help at home, it was no longer enough. Adult day care was the next turn of events. God always gives you what you need. I needed some time for myself and know that mother would get the care she needed. My sister and I took my mother to the day care center. I was like a kindergarten parent leaving my child. I thought, "Oh no. Here we go again, strange people and new surroundings."

"Is this where my mother belongs?" I asked myself. Many of these people are struggling to walk. They have difficulty hearing, can't see clearly and seem confused. But my sister agreed this was where she belonged. It was a touch of reality and one we were afraid of.

My mother did not want to go, but she was willing to give it a chance. Well, thank God that we did. This is again where God steps in and provides the people to do his work. I could fill a book with the kind words and gentle loving gestures that greeted us. Simple comments made us feel at home: "Mary, the coffee is on. You look so beautiful today. We missed you. How are you and your family?"

When I looked around, I saw people engaged. I watched someone in a wheelchair who could not speak but was smiling. He was having fun catching a ball with an aide. These simple acts gave me peace. I truly felt washed with healing graces when I picked my mother up.

I received an update on my mother's day from her dear friend who had the same name of Mary. She was in a wheelchair due to a stroke. She could speak clearly and only had the use of her right hand. So, of course, that right hand was used for the good of others. She encouraged my mother to eat her food and eagerly gave me a report on what she ate. She wanted a kiss from me. She smiled with her eyes and squeezed my hand tightly. All she wanted was to be helpful. She reminded my mother to try to stand, participate in activities, and not to worry. Her only request for me was to pray for her. I assured her that I would. She was a light to others. I recalled how God sent an angel to watch over my mother at the other senior center, too. I truly believe God is watching over us and sending us people to comfort and support us.

On a Friday, the seniors and the group with disabilities joined together for singing and dancing. Every so often the center would have a prom. It was heartwarming to see the people who felt so loved beaming as they danced while in a wheelchair or simply swayed to the music while holding someone's hand. The glow on their faces spoke volumes. There were no differences in whether you were in a wheelchair, could or could not see. You just felt the peace, joy and kindness.

I spoke to the director one morning, telling her how I was overwhelmed with the love that I felt there. She told me, "I have been working with the people of various disabilities for forty years. Individuals need to be respected and recognized as a person. People need opportunities to learn, no matter what it takes and where they are." Some of the adults that are here were once the babies in her care at another facility. She said something that made me freeze and that was, "This is the passion of Christ."

She said, "We were put on the earth to deliver God's message and we all have a different message to learn and to deliver." The words she repeated were, "Do unto others as you would have them do to you." (Luke 6:31)

As I recall the director's words, this is where you see the passion of Christ. It is Jesus who suffered with loneliness, rejection, isolation, sadness, depression, pain and torment. It is when we join with Jesus and become like him that we can help one another. Jesus was present in the Adult Day Center. I felt it with every fiber of my being.

Thankful through all these *surrenders*, I have been on a mission to tell others of God's great love for us. I believe his grace is simply there for the asking. He is always there for us even if we don't always feel his love or understand it.

**I will praise you, Lord, with all my heart; I
will declare all your wondrous deeds.
(Psalm 9: 2–3)**

My surrender to writing about God's grace intensified when I awoke from a sound sleep in the middle of the night. I marveled at how God's grace flowed from me onto paper. I began writing the following words, "The gold thread is woven through the fabric of my life."

I immediately thought this is not from me. God is sending me a message. Over the next few nights of waking up and writing more, I realized that God is the gold thread in my life. As I age, I see the fabric of my life as a tapestry.

I knew I was taking a glimpse into God's glorious graces. I kept writing.

God's grace is the gold thread which is woven through the fabric of my life.

The tapestry is full of designs and patterns which interconnect.

It is not complicated. It is strong and straight. God's golden thread of grace is always present even when we don't see it or feel it.

It stands out above the busyness. It is brilliant.

It is consistent.

The tapestry has many rough spots which are uncomfortable to touch. It has holes, bumps and places that are worn. Some spots you do not want to touch.

Many other spots are smooth, silky and comforting. There are places where your fingers do not want to leave. The gold thread is the grace of God which is the light that shines through the darkness. It is our strength.

I began seeing how my life was not merely a series of events but well-planned by God. He allowed people and places to define the patterns and designs I needed most.

The tapestry is full of designs and patterns which interconnect.

I discovered that people from my past were there to guide me, and I later learned that there were no coincidences. I recall being in fourth grade when our teacher told us she would miss us over the summer since she did not have children. I sat crying in the classroom as the other children were laughing and thinking of the summer fun ahead. I thought something was wrong with me for being sad. Now I recall the words that were told to me by a religious sister at an early age. She told me that I was given the gift of empathy. I saw that I could feel so deeply for others and that feeling is a gift. Throughout my life compassion has been one of the patterns that I see connecting me to others.

It is not complicated. It is strong and straight. God's golden thread of grace is always present even when we don't see it or feel it.

I look back at my early years and do not see failure as I once did. They were opportunities to grow and be strengthened with God's grace. I smile as I hold onto the crucifix around my neck. When I was young, my parents bought it for me in Florence, Italy. I have rarely taken it off and I have been told many times that the gold shines so brightly. It is the gold thread which has been woven through my life. It is Jesus.

All of us who wrote our life-altering experiences in this book have been transformed by God's grace. Reflecting on our lives, we praise God for these graces. Working together on this book, our lives have been connected—threads interweaving in God's tapestry. I do not know what lies ahead, but I do know our God is full of love and mercy. Reflect on your own life and allow his limitless love to surround you and fill your life with his graces.

Moments of Grace

Are there times when you question where God is and why he does not take away the anguish and suffering in your life?

Do you believe that God knows what is best for you?

Are you willing to surrender your soul to God?

Do you find peace and joy in knowing that God is a God of love and mercy?

Prayer

Dear Lord, I ask you to help me to trust in you.
I want to surrender my life to you.
You knew me even before I was born. You know my every thought.
Please shower me with your graces. Help me to do your will.
I hope to help others since we are all
connected by God's immense love.
Thank you for loving me beyond my comprehension.

CHAPTER 2

BECOME LIKE A CHILD

For sixteen years I taught kindergarten in a Catholic school, and I told hundreds of children that God loves them and has a purpose for them. Children are amazing teachers. Their message is simple and that is to love. They understand that God is love and it all comes from him. When they ask for help, they believe God will give them what they need. They like to laugh, imagine and wonder at the simple gifts of creation. They have a great trust in God, they pray for those suffering, and they have a desire to help in any way they can. For children, trusting comes naturally.

As adults, trusting in God is not easy because we want to be in charge. We easily place trust in people, money, material things and, most of all, ourselves. The children followed the caring guidance of their parents and teachers. They were open to following someone outside of themselves.

Even though I did not always feel it, I knew that God was guiding me and providing me with what I needed at the time. I remember as a child being alone in the back of the church. I must have been eight years old. I told God how very much I loved him. I remember being showered with a tremendous love that felt like oceans and oceans of love being poured out. As a child, I talked to God about myself and my family. The seeds of trusting in someone beyond myself were there.

I struggled through school. I remember names were called out with test results at the end of a school year, and I usually was next to the bottom of the list. The teacher said, "You made it again by the skin of your teeth." You can imagine how I felt in front of my classmates.

Tutors and summer school were part of my life. I knew I was not considered very bright but believed that God had a purpose for me as he does for everyone. I was accepted into college as a special student. With perseverance and a desire to teach children, I graduated with a degree in Early Childhood.

After much soul-searching, I began to see how my life was not merely a series of events but well-planned by God. He sets people, places and events in my life to allow me to grow in his love. I discovered people from my past were there to guide me, including my kindergarten children. I have learned there are no coincidences.

I truly believe that God is my Father and I am his child. It is not meant to be complicated. He loves me beyond my earthly comprehension. How am I so sure of God's love? I just have to place myself as a child in the back of that church talking to God and I know I have been graced. Scripture reinforces that love to me.

> **For I know well the plans I have in mind for you … plans for your welfare and not for woe, so to give you a future of hope. When you call me, and come and pray to me, you will find me. Yes, when you seek me with all your heart, I will let you find me....**
> **(Jeremiah 29:11–14)**

After teaching young children and raising my own, I listened to children's ideas. As a grandmother, I still marvel at how children think about things. Children have a pure heart. It is not tainted by the world at this early age. Their hearts are open to loving and giving. For them, there is no greater joy than to love and be loved. I delighted watching how easily the children made friends and quickly held hands. They noticed when someone was left out and easily included that person. If you were hurt, they ran to you. If you cried, you were not left alone. If someone lost a loved one or a pet, they made you a card or gave you a hug. Maybe we need a refresher course in these simple but childlike ways.

I shared with the children during our morning circle time that our dog of sixteen years passed away the night before. I, of course, could not act like it was a normal morning. So I told the children that our dog died last night and then I began to cry. I could not speak. A boy who had lost his mother raised his hand. I called on him and he told me not to worry. He told me God was caring for his mother and he will care for my dog, too. He let me know that his mother was watching over him. I cried more. There was very little talking after this conversation. In that brief silence, my consolation came from the mouth of a child.

Just as Jesus is open and sensitive to the needs of others, so were my students. I saw so many acts of kindness in the classroom. Some stand out above the others. One boy came to school after many eye surgeries and was struggling. I watched the tender caring support from another boy. They would talk, laugh and comfort one another. This encouragement made all the difference. As the year progressed, I marveled at the difference in this one boy's life simply by someone being his friend. I saw how God works through other people and I strive to be like the children, to be a friend to someone in need. People in need are there and I believe we just need to open our eyes.

One young boy sitting in his chair was not joining in our activities on the first day of school. He was so quiet. I did not push him since this was the beginning of his school experience and he needed time. He had his head down on the table. When I inquired if something was wrong, he answered, "When I place my hand on my heart, I know my mom will be thinking of me." He kept his hand on his heart most of the day and that was all the comfort he needed. When life is too confusing or too difficult, I simply place my hand on my heart and I'm reminded that I am not alone and that God loves me. That is the comfort that I need and it was taught so simply through a child.

This is the childlike trust Jesus teaches. As the little child recognized his need for his mother to get through his first day of school, Jesus wants us to recognize that we need him to get through our day. The little boy's simple gesture of his hand over his heart expressed that simple truth of needing someone besides himself.

Amen, I say to you, unless you turn and become like children, you will not enter the kingdom of heaven. Whoever humbles himself like this child is the greatest in the kingdom of heaven. (Matthew 18:3–4)

It sounds so simple to be humble. But in the world in which we live, this is not encouraged. We are called to think of gaining more, getting ahead, climbing the ladder and reaching our goals. It is about helping yourself and not helping one another. Jesus tells us to do just the opposite—empty ourselves and rely on him and not on ourselves. He tells us to love God and one another. Jesus came to serve and not to be served. Like the little children, he was not thinking of his needs but the needs of others. Jesus is the best teacher of humility. Let's learn from him and not the world.

Teachers have the opportunity to be a part of children's daily lives. Sometimes the greatest challenges have nothing to do with their learning the curriculum. Events happen in the world and in their homes that require wisdom beyond a teaching degree. I believe Jesus gave me strength and comfort when it was most needed.

I remember one day of teaching in particular. It did not seem different from any other day until the sky grew very dark. You sensed oncoming danger. Our school was in the path of a tornado and we needed to be safe. It meant being away from the windows. Our entire school gathered in the long, narrow and dark center hallway. The children were frightened but they followed directions. We began praying the rosary as a group, huddled together and whispering our prayers in hope that the storm would not harm us. We began to see the light as the storm passed over us and, thankfully, we walked back to our classrooms. The rosary has always been a comfort to me. The tradition of praying the rosary was passed down to me by my mother and her mother. Mary, Queen of Heaven and Earth, would certainly smile on all these children praying her favorite prayer. The rosary gave us peace, hope and comfort.

One day at a faculty meeting, I was told that a safety procedure called "lock down" would go into effect the next day. Following the meeting, I walked into my classroom and fear came over me. I began praying. I did not believe that I could be calm and help the five-year-old children know that a shooter could be in our building and we just needed to be calm. This was too much for me. I asked Jesus to somehow help me to have peace so that I could pass this peace to the children. Well, the following day I felt so peaceful as I explained what was to happen. I told the children, "We just never know what can happen and we must be prepared. So when you hear a certain message on the loud speaker, you do not need to be afraid. We will all go quietly into our closet and I will read and talk in a whisper until we are told to come out." My aide and I were amazed as the children just took this in stride.

There was humor is this situation since I am hard of hearing and I never heard the message on the loud speaker to come out of the closet. The police officer and the principal opened the door after twenty minutes or so had gone by. They wondered why we were still in the closet. My aide, other teachers and I had quite a few laughs that our time in the closet was much longer than the rest of the school.

During this trial, I asked Jesus for the peace that was needed and it was given to me and the others. This could have been a very upsetting situation. It was transformed by simply praying, "Jesus, I trust in You."

Prayer was how we began and ended each day. But I can tell you that the most touching prayers were those that came during our day. They were spontaneous. You only had to respond to the heart of a child. One child seldom spoke. I did not force him to talk. Months had gone by and he raised his hand. I quickly called on him. He told me that his father put his hand through a glass table last night and needed prayers. He wondered if we could pray for him. I told him with a deep concern that, yes, we would pray for his father.

During afternoon play time, I noticed some of the children walked to our prayer table. I knew they had family problems and I could see those with a heavy heart. They did not see anyone watching. I noticed one girl put her head down and talked to God. It was a reminder to me that I don't need a specific prayer and special words to memorize, just talk to God. He hears us and wants his children to come to him.

I occasionally took my kindergarten students outside to the cement bench in front of the statue of Mary. The statue of Mary was very large and nestled in a stone area covered with plants. It was as if we were protected simply by being in Mary's presence. We would pray one decade of the rosary. The children never complained but came willingly with hearts full of prayer requests. Sometimes they just came with joy to be comforted by our heavenly Mother. As I look back on this time in my life, I believe God was letting me know that my prayers were being taken into his hands. I had a husband with job demands, small children and aging parents. I had daily worries and received great peace in these simple heartfelt prayers.

To honor Martin Luther King, I posted a peace prayer in my classroom in the month of January. I wanted the children to know that we have a choice to be a peacemaker or not. I let the children know of the injustices that took place. It was hard for them to believe that people could be that mean. I hope the seed I planted will remain in their hearts. This is surely what God wants for us all. Just think of the difference we can make if we start treating each other as a precious child of God—each one held in the plan of God.

Before I formed you in the womb, I knew you;
before you were born I dedicated you.
(Jeremiah 1:5)

We don't need to complicate our prayer. The spontaneous prayers are honest and open with nothing held back. This childlike trust is a grace. It is a grace to look beyond our power to a greater power. God is our Father and we are his children. It is so simple to just ask our Father to help someone. I realized that God was teaching me and the others that prayer is speaking from the heart.

Children love hearts. At this early age they know hearts mean love. I had a little girl who came from a big family with lots of love but little money. On the last day of school, I received many beautiful packages and her gift was a painting of a heart. This was presented to me in such a loving way. This gift touched my heart more than the others. God taught me that the best gifts are those given from the heart. A child's heart is so pure. Love is all they really want. A child knows that God is love and seeks this love for himself and for others. They understand that God is the giver and that we must ask and he will pour out his love.

A clean heart create for me, God; renew within me a steadfast spirit.
(Psalm 51:12)

Children live in the present moment. They have a great sense of wonder and imagination. Being a full-day kindergarten teacher gave me the opportunity to join in their wonder of exploring everyday things. They can examine the details of a leaf or a bug and then turn it into something magical.

Frequently I heard the children's images of heaven. I kept a notebook and will share some of the children's thoughts:

"Where does earth end and heaven begin?"

"How does God understand all the languages?"

"How does God make the world so lovable?"

"Does God live in the clouds or in your heart?"

"Today is my grandfather's birthday and he is an angel."

"I save half my seat for my guardian angel."

"I want to be a rainbow-watcher when I grow up because I can thank God."

"Some people close their doors but my door is wide open."

"Thunder is when the angels go bowling."

"How does God make lightning?"

"Heaven is where everyone is happy."

"We can eat anything we want in heaven."

"Our animals are waiting for us in heaven."

As I was the observer, I could hear the children tell of their thoughts of heaven. I found comfort in their thoughts. To the children, heaven was filled with love and everything you could imagine that was happy and joyful. They have not been on earth very long but surely can give us hope.

**What eye has not seen, and ear has not heard,
and what has not entered the human heart, what
God has prepared for those who love him.
(1 Corinthians 2:9)**

When a child's life is shortened on earth, it has a major impact on the lives of many souls. For me, the life of Ian Miller was a model of a child's trust in God. Ian was the grandson of my father's cousin. He was twelve years old. He was an active and energetic boy involved in many activities. He was in a sledding accident and passed at this time. In his boot was the scripture:

Consider it pure joy, my brothers, when you face trials of many kinds. Because you know that the testing of your faith develops perseverance. Perseverance must finish its work so you may be mature and complete, not lacking in anything.
(James I:2–4 *New International Version*)

At his Celebration of Life, his grandmother said to me, "I would not be standing here if not for the grace of God." I was so moved by her strength but knew this was from God.

Ian's parents set up an organization called "In Ian's Boots." They send shoes and boots with the scripture message all around the world. In partnering with another organization, 13,000 pairs of shoes were sent to Haiti so that the children could enter school.

His mother developed a lung disease after her only son's passing. She told me, "God is our strength. I speak without notes. The words just come out. It can be preschool to college and the message is always the same. It is miraculous. Even though my husband and I miss our son terribly, we want to be good stewards of God's work. When we see our son in heaven, he will ask us, 'What took you so long to get here?'"

Ian carried the word of God in his heart as well as in his boot. Keep the word of God close. Let it be a part of you. His short time on earth showed us that trials will come. We need to trust God and realize that he is in control. He sees the bigger picture and cares about our souls. We look for life to be easy, comfortable, and to be in control. Let us know that God works all things for a greater good.

At Ian's Celebration of Life many tears were shed. I watched my aunt hug her cousin, who was Ian's grandfather. She and he did not let go for a very long time. My aunt had lost her twenty-two-year-old son. He was stationed in Hawaii. He was in the Para Rescue Division of the United States Air Force and was attempting to save a man with a bleeding ulcer. The high winds caused the helicopter to crash. I will never forget the pain and anguish of the family during the funeral. It was a 21-gun salute tribute to my cousin. What stands out most to me is the faith and grace that God bestowed upon the family. My aunt knows that God gives us what we need when we need it. She was able to accept this as God's will. He sees the bigger picture. It is not what we want. God graces us with strength to carry us when the suffering is too much to bear.

We never know when our time will come. Time is of the essence. Every choice we make has a consequence. God can change our hearts. I know that I do not have what it takes to always be kind, loving and patient. I must keep asking for help.

To bring Jesus to others is very simple and is not complicated. It is giving love in the hugs, smiles, kind words and listening to another. It is being there when someone needs you—encouraging, giving hope, joy and, most of all, the love that we are all in need of. We are here to serve the needs of others.

A child is no different than an adult when it comes to suffering. We all experience sickness and weakness at one time or another. Children immediately see the need to assist and comfort another. I had a girl in my classroom that had an illness that required frequent visits to the hospital. While she was gone, the children prayed for her, wrote her cards, drew pictures, role-played what it must have felt like to be in a hospital.

When she returned to the classroom, she was showered with kindness and love that I was privileged to observe. I watched the children show such compassion and empathy. It comes so natural. This young child showed the others how to deep breathe, relax, laugh and be comforted as she had learned in the hospital. I was a silent observer of role-playing the situations that helped this child through many difficult periods of illness. The children gathered around her so eagerly to learn how to care for another. It was beautiful to see!

I was blessed to have had an aide to share my faith. She and I frequently watched the loving actions of the children in our care. My aide had heartache of her own. Her husband became very ill and needed to be in the hospital for long periods of time. She had to travel a long distance to get there. She let me know that she would run to get there each day whatever the weather. Many at our school and community prayed the rosary for her husband and the family. When her husband passed, I recall thousands attended his funeral to show their respect and admiration. He truly was a humble follower of Jesus. He accepted his suffering graciously. Instead of thinking of himself, he comforted those around him. He always had the rosary in his hand, knowing that Jesus and Mary were giving him the strength. Their love for one another was and is an inspiration to many. My aide came back to work to be with the children since she knew their love would comfort and support her through her sorrow.

A child has an amazing ability to bounce back from difficult times. They quickly see the lighter side of life. Their laughter is one of the most joyful noises on the planet. We have so much to learn from the children.

Moments of Grace

There is a reason that Jesus wants us to become like children. It is simple. They know how to love, trust, laugh, be joyful, wonder, be a friend, help others and live simply. They do not worry about tomorrow. They live in the present and one that is full of hope.

Prayer

Dear God, please open my heart
to be loving, kind, compassionate and as caring as a child.
Help me to be joyful, wonder, laugh, hope, and trust in you.
Let me never forget that we are all your precious children.
Help me to treat others as I would want to be treated.

Meeting Elisa

Sister Janice made the connection between Elisa and I. It was all part of God's plan. I have been profoundly changed by knowing Elisa. I am convinced that God has a purpose for each of our lives. Elisa is a living miracle of God's immense love for us.

As a lay missionary of the Sacred Heart, she is called to be the heart of God in the world wherever she is needed, whether with her family, parish ministries or the Kairos Prison Ministry. Her latest evangelization endeavor is her website, heavenhelpus.net, which offers a place where one can explore the many ways heaven is trying to help us!

She will teach you how to forgive and it is only because of God. She is an open vessel to the will of God. She will comfort you and inspire you to know that you are never alone, even in the darkest times of your life. Allow Elisa to show you the way to experience joy amidst suffering.

CHAPTER 3

FOLLOW THE GRACE

**For by grace you have been saved through faith;
and that not of yourselves, it is the gift of God;
not as a result of works, so that no one may boast.
(Ephesians 2:8–9)**

S omeone once asked me, "Elisa, what do you want carved on your tombstone?" My immediate response was, "Everything Is A Grace." These words were given to us by St. Therese of Lisieux. She spoke them in teachings to her novices and wrote them in letters to her sisters and also in her own personal notebooks. Therese gave me the words my heart did not know how to speak. They sum up what I believe about myself and my life—everything in my life is a grace.

It may help you to understand how I came to adopting those words as my own, by telling you a bit about myself and why these words affect so deeply how I live my life. Everything is a surprise to me. I take nothing for granted. Everything is a grace, an unmerited gift of God's extravagant love for me. I did not always know this because of all the abuse I endured as a child, but I do now.

I need to add a bit of a cautionary note here. I was asked to do this because the stories of abuse, at the hands of my parents that I wrote about, are difficult to read. I wrote these stories to show what God and his grace can do for and with a life. I do this only to give glory to God and to help heal the heart of another. In an effort to add a bit of balm to the heart before I begin, I will tell you how things ended. Everything you will read has been forgiven. Jesus himself did this in me, with me and for me. I did none of it on my own.

Due to his alcoholism, my father ended up living a solitary life for many years before his passing in March, 2014. In his later years I saw him a few times and he was quite respectful to me. During our last encounter at my brother's house, my father said very little to me. He would just look over at me with a brief glance but that look told me volumes. Our Lord allowed me to see my father wasn't the same person anymore. I could see a glimpse of the sorrow in his heart for all he had done to me when I was a child.

The same thing happened with my mother. During my adult years after having children, my mother and I did just fine. My mother was a fantastic cook and baker and we had this joy of cooking in common. I inherited her personal hand-written cookbook of treasured recipes when she died. My mom had a great sense of humor. I'd like to think I inherited some of that from her. My mom was a terrific grandmother. As far as my children were concerned she was just mom-mom ... lots of fun and they could always count on amazing meals when they went to her house for a visit.

In my mother's later years, when she was quite ill, our Lord allowed me to see her heroic virtue during her illness while taking her to her doctor appointments. Jesus showed me the same thing that he showed me with my father. My mother wasn't the same person anymore. The two people who abused me so terribly as a child didn't exist. What they had done in their young adult years was not who they were. It was what they had done. Now that said, you might want to buckle up before reading any further. Just know for certain, God's grace has covered all of it. For my part, as I write, I do my best to follow the grace I am given.

The first moment I clearly remember tangibly experiencing God's grace was when I was seven years old. My father threw me down the cellar steps after he tried to drown me in the bathtub. The first two times he held my head at the bottom of the tub, my instincts took over and I fought him with every ounce of strength I had in me. The water hitting my head really added to my terror. He would pull me up out of the water just seconds before I took in too much water and drowned.

By the third time my father did this I had had it. I vividly remember the moment I made this decision. Dying seemed like a good idea to me. Dying was definitely better than the brutality of my father. I stopped fighting. I just didn't have anymore fight in me. I was completely exhausted and let myself go. As I felt myself drowning, I had this wonderful peace flood through me under the water. I didn't feel the water pounding my head anymore from the spigot above, nor my hair being wrenched in my father's fist while he held me under the water. I no longer heard the horrible and venomous guttural screams coming from him that just moments before sickened and terrified me. It was over. I was floating in a warm, sweet and silent peace. For a few seconds I rested in this serene sense of peace and inner calm.

Moments later I was cruelly yanked out of the water. My father shook me violently as I choked and gasped for air. I didn't grasp what was happening right away. All I could see was the horror on my father's face as he realized he had almost killed me. I had actually frightened him. I knew it. This brutal and diabolical monster that was my father felt a moment of fear. This moment was not lost on me. Even at seven years of age I took a tiny bit of satisfaction in this. For me, it was a small victory.

My shred of victory was short-lived. What came next was rage, sickening and diabolical rage. That is when my father threw me down the hallway like a bowling ball where I slid all the way into the bedroom at the end of the hall. I crash-landed under the bed with the bedsprings scraping my wet naked body as I flew under them. My father came after me, screaming. He pulled me out from under the bed and dragged me by my hair back down the hallway, then down the steps to the first floor, through the house, to the top of the cellar and threw me down the steps to the concrete floor below.

I was banished to our basement, buck naked, soaking wet, cold, shaking and terrified. I found an old, dirty and what was at one time white towel with a wide navy blue stripe down the center of it with the word K-LINE imprinted on it. I wrapped myself in the towel and sat on some trash bags filled with old clothes that were in an empty coal bin. I sat in there until I calmed down a bit. I passed the time just sitting there. When I was thirsty I drank out of the spigot from the wash tub. I also found some Coke syrup in a jug on a shelf. It was really thick and sweet but good. I rooted around in an old metal cabinet and found what looked like chocolate-covered pretzels. I found out later they were dog pretzels. I ate some of those. They were good. They tasted like they had vitamins in them. We used to have a jar of chewable Flintstone vitamins sitting on the kitchen counter. Those little pretzels tasted a little like they were ground up in there and covered in chocolate to hide the taste. Not too bad.

Something else happened while I was down in that basement. All fear left me completely. I somehow knew I was not alone. As I sat on the bottom cellar step, I could feel this presence in me. It was with me, comforting and helping me. I have never forgotten that presence within me that day. I held onto this knowledge and peace within me the same as one would hold onto a person. Put an image in your mind of when you were a child of about seven years old. Imagine you are holding hands with a friend as you walk and talk and laugh in the carefree way children do. That is the image that never leaves me when I remember that time in the basement. I knew I was not alone. I was being held and protected by a presence I could tangibly feel but, at the time, could not see or name. The sweetness of that image still rests in my heart and mind.

This extraordinary grace in my life began much earlier though, even before I was born. From my first moments after taking my first breath, in a small third-floor apartment, I was in serious trouble. I was born three months too soon. My mother did not realize she was still pregnant. Several months before, she had gone to a doctor to undo the whole thing. She had an abortion.

The morning I was born my mother was on her way to the bathroom. The pressure she felt was not what she thought. She was stricken with terror when she looked down and saw she was pushing out a baby. My mother told me she began screaming for my father to come and get her. Just minutes before she had been in the kitchen making breakfast. My father carried her back to the bedroom. He didn't realize right away what was happening. They both looked down in horror as my mother delivered me the rest of the way herself. That is how I came into this world.

After arriving at the hospital, doctors told my parents two things: pick a name for her and call a priest to have her baptized because she will not survive the day. My father yelled at the doctors and my mother that no one was to name me until he got back. He walked out of the hospital and straight to the nearest bar where he called my grandmother to ask her to send a priest to the hospital. He sat down at the bar to drink and think of a name. While there, the song *Mona Lisa* came over the radio. My father jumped up and ran back to the hospital. From that song he came up with the name Elisa.

My name means consecrated to God or House of God. I am sure my father did not know this. God did. I'm thinking God knew someday this knowledge would console me and that, no matter what happened to me, I was to know for certain I belonged to him. This was the information I would need to hold in my heart at all times ... to survive.

At about the same time each year, I would know what was coming. My mother would come in from work sometime after 2 a.m. and tell me to make her a drink because "I have to tell you something." She would then recount every detail of how she thought she ended my life in her womb.

Knowing my mother tried to end my life in her womb was awful. That was not the worst part. For me, it was what my mother told me incessantly until I wished I *had* died. She point-blank told me that what tormented her mind most was that she just could not figure out how I ever survived! She would go over every detail in order of how it all happened from the moment she went into the bathroom to how she hemorrhaged for weeks after her abortion. My mother would look at me like I was an alien and, with a tortured look on her face, ask me over and over in her drunken state, "How did you survive?" This is the question that haunted her. She would ask me this question until she passed out from drinking too much.

What a shame I did not know what to say to her back then. I could have eased her tormented mind. I didn't know to tell her that God had a plan. The love of God had a plan for me for a future and a hope. His plan was for me to live. That is the answer to the question, "How did you survive?" That was a plan my mother could never conceive of nor accept. She told me repeatedly that I was her penance in life. I was the punishment for the sin she had committed.

During my childhood my parents made it very clear to me that I was not wanted and that my very presence was a source of pain and revulsion for them. Both my mother and father would scream at me quite often, in fits of anger, that the very sight of me made them sick. Knowing this nearly crushed my spirit.

My mother's anger reached a boiling point one night when, in a deluge of rage, she nearly strangled me to death. That was another night that the very sight of me made her sick. I was fifteen years old at the time. As my mother was strangling me, I could feel myself dying. The demonic look of hatred in her eyes as she looked into mine was horrible. That tormented look, asking yet again, "How did you survive?" That night I almost didn't.

It is an odd sensation to know you are dying. At one point I fought back as hard as I could during all the madness, screaming and terror. At another point I just stopped and allowed myself to be enveloped in the interior calm that took over. That is the moment my brother and my sister succeeded in pulling my mother off me. They realized she was actually killing me.

I think when it was all over my mother was horrified at what she had done. I think she scared herself. I know in my heart that all the guilt she allowed to torment her for so many years over what she had done in trying to abort me was unleashed that night as she tried to strangle me. The hatred for me that I saw in her eyes with the question ... how did you survive? ... was completely spent.

It was only God's divine intervention and grace that allowed me to survive the brutal attacks, beatings and abuse of every kind during my childhood and years growing up. This abuse continued until the night I just wrote about. From that point on, I never experienced any kind of abuse in any way from either parent.

You are reading this particular chapter, "Follow the Grace," because Barbara Arbuckle read an unpublished book I wrote called, *Then, I Look At The Cross.* After reading this book, Barbara asked me if I would contribute my thread to the tapestry of her book. She asked me to answer two questions: How do I define the grace of God? And what does God's grace mean to me?

I thought these would be very easy questions to answer. Everything I have ever written has been my response to God's grace. It was his grace that allowed me to write. What's so difficult about that? Apparently everything! I had so many technical difficulties with my computer that made it impossible to get any writing accomplished.

We have a silly thing in our family that my sister Barb invented. She calls it the *Tuesday Surprise*. Barb has determined that surprises come on Tuesdays. She is so often correct that it is amazing. This Tuesday was no different. I was in for a very big surprise this particular evening. It is my routine on Tuesdays to attend a rosary novena at a nearby church. I was in such a miserable mood this night I planned to stay home. I had two questions to answer, remember? I made one last attempt at putting something down on paper but my computer kept shutting down, so I decided to go to the novena.

As we were praying the second sorrowful mystery, a light caught my eye. The light was coming from a statue of Our Lady holding baby Jesus in her arms. Only it wasn't a statue anymore. It became part of the light and turned in my direction. The light felt like a magnet of peace between the image and myself. I heard a very soft interior voice speak these words:

Grace is God restoring all things through Christ who died to save everyone.
In my mind's eye I could see this acronym.

Grace is:

God
Restoring
All things through
Christ who died to save
Everyone

Earlier this day I had wailed to heaven, "Lord, where is your grace!?" It wasn't a question. I hollered it in a fit of frustration. I had allowed the events of the day to rattle me so badly that I forgot what I have always known and held in my heart—everything is a gift of God's grace and his unconditional, abiding love.

God's grace is always there for the asking. I was not really asking for his help. I wanted things my way and according to my timetable and I was relying on my efforts. Since that didn't happen, I grudgingly went to the novena. While there, I did quiet myself and in prayer ask our Lord to forgive me. I asked Jesus and Mary to help me with my writing. Prayer changes things. Thank you, Mother Mary and baby Jesus, for this gift of untying that really big knot! Thank you for telling me and showing me in those heaven-sent words the meaning of grace.

Another thing happened to me that night. I received another *Tuesday Surprise.* Maybe this was my guardian angel. Who knows? It was, however, from heaven trying to help me. Even though I had such a wonder-filled experience in church, I was still feeling miserable from the earlier awful part of the day. I crawled into bed and pulled the covers over my head, happy to have the day finally over. As I was falling asleep, I heard these words whispered in my ear, **Grace is spiritual air.** These words were clear as a bell and hit my heart with such a sweet warmth like a bear hug from God. Thank you, Lord! I fell asleep that night snug as a bug in that spiritual air!

So what is this spiritual air that was whispered to me as I was falling asleep that night? I think this spiritual air is the grace our souls need to live. Our souls are animated by God's grace. As scripture says, "For in him we live and move and have our being...." (Acts 17:28) whether we are here on earth or in our eternal home. Our souls will live forever.

"Follow the grace" are words that have lived in my heart for many years. They were the words of a dear friend, spiritual mentor and guide. I met her when we lived in New York. We would often sit in her apartment over a cup of tea, sharing our faith, our lives and love for God with each other. During our last visit before I moved to Georgia, she leaned into my car and said, "Elisa, remember to *follow the grace.*"

These words have never left me. I have reflected on this piece of advice many times over the past several years. When I began this piece of writing, I was not following the grace. I was not listening to God or waiting for him to tell me what I needed to write. I had my agenda and my timetable. I can't think a thought or write a word or anything else for that matter until I am given the grace to do it. Nothing was possible until I followed the grace he gave me.

How do I define the grace of God? You know my answer already. Just like St. Therese, I believe "Everything is a grace." It is what Our Lady allowed me to know while praying the rosary.

Grace is **God restoring all things through Christ** who died to save everyone.

No matter what the circumstance, God's grace is there. We have a great big God who loves all of us without limits. He is a marvelous God who lavishes his grace on us abundantly. It is up to us to open our hearts to receive it.

What does grace mean to me? As was whispered in my ear as I was falling asleep, *Grace is spiritual air.* Grace is the spiritual air I need to breathe for the life of my soul. It allows me to navigate through my life on earth with God, holding his hand, as I journey through faith to the next life—eternal life with HIM. I guess how successful I am on this journey is determined by how well I listen to the spiritual wisdom given to us by St. Therese of Lisieux in *The Yellow Notebook*:

> Everything is a grace, everything is the direct effect of our Father's Love— difficulties, contradictions, humiliations, all the soul's miseries, her burdens, her needs, everything, because through them, she learns humility, realizes her weakness. Everything is a grace because everything is God's gift. Whatever be the character of life or its unexpected events—to the heart that loves, all is well.

Moments of Grace

I have determined that God interrupts our lives with moments of grace at the exact moment we need them. These moments of grace bolster our faith and help us to trust in God as we experience his love and care for us. As you read my story, were you thinking of your own? As you read about the graces I received during some very difficult times, were you reminded of what God has done for you as well? How has God interrupted your life with moments of grace? These two questions would be good topics for personal reflection and conversation with a close friend.

Everyone has a story and a story to tell. Our stories lift each other up. They give us encouragement and hope. They connect us ... one to another ... much more deeply for having shared them. What's your story? I invite you to share your story when the opportunity presents itself for the purpose of lifting the other and showing how God has interrupted your life with a moment of grace that helped you ... caused you to know he was with you ... loving you. You will both be blessed!

Prayer

Dear Abba Father, we present ourselves to you that you may anoint us with your Holy Spirit. May our hearts be filled with your grace to see others through your eyes and love them with your love. Filled with your Spirit, may we follow your grace to help heal the hearts of those you place in our path and draw them closer to you. May we do these things through the United Hearts of Jesus and Mary, all for your glory! Amen

CHAPTER 4

IT ALL BEGAN WITH LOVE

**Just as the Father has loved me, I have
also loved you; remain in my love.
(John 15:9)**

"Fall in love with God! He's madly in love with you!"

I wish with all my heart that every single one of you was sitting next to me the day I heard these words! I was sitting in church waiting for my pastor to begin his homily when he walked down from the altar and into the aisle as he proclaimed these words. He was standing right next to me when he said them.

"Fall in love with God! He's madly in love with you!"

I have absolutely no idea what he said next! I don't remember much else from that homily. I think I was holding my breath. I sat there stunned. These words hit my heart like a hammer hitting a gong. They just kept reverberating over and over in my heart and mind. I questioned his words immediately. *What is he talking about? How is this possible? Is this really true?* Though I hadn't experienced it, my heart knew what he said was true. And that was only the beginning.

For the past eighteen years since I heard that homily, God has been showing me how he has always loved me. God has been showing me by every means possible what he knows will get my attention. He does this through all the seemingly random people who cross my path, the sights and sounds of nature, music, events, homilies, books, prayer time, encounters with family and friends—the list is endless. All of it is planned by God to show me his love and care.

Even when I was being abused and was my most-shattered and broken, I was loved by God. Just because I didn't know it or feel his love did not mean it wasn't true. It just meant I didn't know it or feel it. It is the same for each of us. God loves every single one of us as if we were the only person on earth and so much more than we can possibly imagine. No matter who you are or what you have done, that statement is true. God is love. He can do nothing else but love.

Allow me to share a few of the ways God has revealed his love to me. He taught me how to forgive those who abused me. You see it wasn't just at the hands of my parents. There were many people who hurt me in this way. It is only a miracle of God's grace that all of it didn't kill me—heart, mind, body and soul. It is not necessary to write all of it. What I want you to know is that all of it has been forgiven. My prayer is that as you continue reading, you will be reminded of how God has intervened in your own life in your dark moments. God did this for me one day through a counselor, a friend, a cell phone and a song ... and a visit from his Son.

Several times over the years I have sought professional help to negotiate through all the videos in my head. It was on one of those days that God intervened so tenderly to comfort me. One day in my counselor's office I was, with his help, trying to work through a particularly harrowing day of abuse that happened when I was five years old. I had been walking around with this video in my head for almost fifty years. I had never told a living soul about it until this day in my counselor's office. I had always thought that the process of actually telling someone would mean I had to relive all of it over again. I did not understand at the time that that is not so.

I wish I could tell you that the most awful thing my father had ever done to me was to lock me in a basement or try to drown me in a bathtub. It was not. On this particular day he had something more heinous in mind. He tied me down to the kitchen table, tying my arms and legs to the table legs, in order to torture me with things he had sitting on the table. It was a morning of terror and agony for me. When my father was finished what he was doing, he stood me on a stool in front of the kitchen sink so I could wash all the things he used to torment me. When I was finished he sent me off to kindergarten. In those days I was old enough to walk to school by myself. It was a miracle that I did not go insane that day.

I have another memory of this day that Jesus showed me while in my counselor's office. I can play this video in my head anytime I want. It is always there to console me. I remember looking over in the corner of the kitchen and Jesus was standing there. He walked out from the corner of the kitchen and knelt down next to me. He knelt right next to the kitchen table and, without saying a word, leaned his head next to mine. He rested his forehead right next to the side of my face. That was enough. That was more than enough. Once you see Jesus and feel his presence, there is peace. Everything else falls away. Jesus could not stop my father from hurting me but he could help me through it. It was Jesus who gave me the strength to survive that day.

Even though I did not have to relive the horror of that day with my counselor, what had happened to me was still difficult. After I left his office, I sat in my car for a few minutes to compose myself before I drove home. Before I pulled away, I checked my cell phone. There was a photo message sent to me from a friend. I opened the file and there was a picture of Jesus. Under the photo of Jesus in the Blessed Sacrament was the message, "I'm praying for you." The entire time I was in the counselor's office, my friend was in her parish chapel 1,400 miles away, praying for me.

That is not all. As I started to drive away I turned on my CD player. The song playing was *Angel Rays* by Sissel. The song talks about the difficult road of a child and how "this child of mine, she'll forever shine ... angel rays watch over you." I had no doubt that God's angel rays were watching over me that day.

There is more. Just a couple of weeks later I asked a friend at a prayer meeting to pray over me. She did and then told me these words. She said Jesus showed her a terrible scene. She saw me as a little girl tied to a table. Jesus would not allow her to see what was happening to me. She said she could hear me screaming. She told me that there were angels above me and their rays were pouring over me and that Jesus was with me!

I never told her what had happened to me. I still haven't told her the details of that day. She did see, however, the angel rays that were watching over me. Have I forgiven my father all of that? Yes. Jesus himself gave me the grace to forgive it. I did none of that on my own.

My next lesson in forgiveness came while reading Caryll Houselander's *Essential Writings*. In the second chapter, "Mystical Body," she described in vivid detail a vision she was given by Jesus of how he lives in each person. She saw Jesus living, dying, sorrowing and rejoicing in them. Jesus showed her that some are dead to his presence in them. They are his tombs and we must comfort him in them because he is the life of their soul.

As I read the account of this vision, I was stunned by the beauty of it, truly the wonder of what it must mean to know Jesus lives in us in such a profoundly intimate and unitive way. As I read Houselander's words, I could literally feel the meaning of them wash over me. That meant that, during one of the most horrific experiences of my entire life, I was not alone. Jesus was with me. As I came to this realization, I was filled with such a love for God I could barely breathe. This love permeated every fiber of my being. It was the heart of God himself filling me with his love that gave me the desire, courage and strength to forgive some of the most diabolical acts that could be done to a child. It all happened in a flash. I saw the entire experience in that moment with one very big difference. This time Jesus was there and he showed me how he was there.

When I was nine years old, I spent an entire afternoon being beaten and brutalized by my father in ways that almost killed me. If I wrote everything that happened, you wouldn't be able to read the words. If I did that, I would be hurting you with what was done to me. I have chosen love. Only love heals. I have decided to use my pain to help others heal.

As I read Houselander's words, Jesus showed me how he was living in me and in my father at the very same time. He showed me how he experienced every drop of abuse and horror. Nothing happened to me that did not happen to him. He lived it with me, in me. He also lived what was happening in my father. Jesus suffered all of it.

The entire time my father was abusing me, Jesus suffered beyond my ability to convey in human words. Both my father and I were his children. He was loving me and keeping me alive the entire time. Jesus was also doing everything he could to prompt my father to stop what he was doing. Jesus showed me how he was loving us both infinitely all at the very same time. Jesus was trying to LOVE my father into stopping the horror.

I witnessed Jesus suffer the agony of my father choosing evil over his love! I experienced how deeply he loved me and what he did to try and save me from the abuse. He couldn't interfere with my father's free will so he endured all of it. He took it on himself so I would not be alone. With Jesus, I forgave my father everything.

I saw what Caryll Houselander wrote about the reverence we must have for a sinner and how we can comfort Christ who is suffering in that sinner. In my father, Jesus was living in agony. How can one see this and not forgive? This is a way I can comfort Christ. I can forgive. This is also the reason I wrote why some of my abuse has to remain hidden. I can understand a bit how Jesus suffers in those people. I can be there for Jesus the way he was for me so many years ago in my father. I can return Jesus' love for me and comfort him with his love!

Houselander also saw how Christ in the tomb is potentially the risen Christ. We all have loved ones where Christ is suffering in them. We are never to lose hope or give up on them. While we are waiting and praying for that day, for the day Jesus rises from the tomb in them, we can continue to pray and sacrifice for them.

After I finished writing the words you just read, I stopped to go and set up for Adoration at our parish church. I blessed myself with holy water as I walked out the door. I heard these words in my heart: *Offer all of this as a sacrifice of praise to my glory!* I knew what Jesus was asking me. This is how I could comfort him. I could hold all of it in my heart in silence. I could give him all my pain, everything I have suffered and be an offering of praise to his greater glory! So there was Jesus offering me a way to allow him to create a greater good out of what was done to me. He could use all of it to help others heal for his greater glory. Amen!

As you have just read, with God's grace I have been able to forgive so much of the abuse I endured as a child. You may be surprised to learn, however, that I battle so fiercely the temptation not to forgive! Jesus knows this also. While at Mass one day, I was grieving deeply a horrible act of abuse that totally blindsided me. I think this is why it hurt so badly. It happened right after the day of diabolical abuse I wrote about at the hands of my father.

Soon after that day, both parents abandoned all seven of us. We lived in the house alone for days. Our grandmother found out and sent family members to pick us up and bring us to her house. I thought I was being rescued! To my horror I was not. I was abused there as well, that very day, by another family member in the same way my father abused me. My nine-year-old spirit was crushed. I could barely breathe. My mind was reeling with the knowledge that I was not safe ... anywhere. This person threatened me that, if I told my grandmother, they would make sure my brothers and sisters and I would be put in an orphanage. I remained silent and broken. I know I have forgiven this act of violence against me, yet the memory is still there.

I think "Old Red Legs" (that's what I call the evil one) reminds us of these things and throws them in our face with such venom and cruelty. He was right there, tempting me and reminding me of every detail of the abuse. Don't forgive! Don't forgive! Jesus was with me as well when the Psalm 34:18 was read, "The Lord is close to the broken-hearted and saves the crushed in spirit." Jesus was there in his word to comfort me. He reminded me not to believe the "Father of Lies" and that, yes, all of this has been forgiven though the memory remains. I offered the Mass that day for the person who abused me in such a disgusting way. I added this prayer to my offering. *Bless them Lord, change me.*

After Mass I knelt before the tabernacle for a few minutes of thanksgiving for the Eucharist I just received, that blessed moment of union with God. As I looked up at the statue of Mary above the tabernacle, her arms were open wide. Her hands were pointing down in the direction of the tabernacle where Jesus lives for love of us. Mary does what she always does and points us to her son.

I smiled up at her as I remembered an acronym she gave me a couple of months back. That day, Mother Mary and her open arms were trying to comfort me as well. She knows the depth of my wounds. Even healed wounds leave a scar.

The acronym is Mary herself.

M.A.R.Y.

M: Mass ... stay close to Jesus in the Holy Mass.

A: Adoration ... adore my son in his Most Blessed Sacrament. He is waiting for you. His presence will heal you.

R: Read God's word. Reconcile yourselves to my son and pray the rosary I gave you.

Y: Yes ... say yes to Jesus and do whatever he tells you. I will help you. Always.

With Mary holding my hand to guide me to her son and Jesus holding the other, my intention is to do whatever he tells me.

What is that, Lord? What is it that you want me to do with all you have given me? I prayed that God would use me to help others heal as well. On June 30, 2000, Jesus showed me one way I could do this. I made a commitment to share in the charism of the Missionary Sisters of the Sacred Heart. The entire charism of this Sacred Heart Family is "Called to be the heart of God in the world." This charism is at the center of everything I do. My intention is to be God's heart in the world for others, for all he desires to encounter through me.

Soon after making this commitment, my husband's job transferred us to New York state where I first became involved in prison ministry. A small group of us went to the justice center each week for a Bible study and to teach and pray the rosary with the men and women incarcerated there.

While ministering at this facility, we encountered a serial killer. This was a man accused of raping and murdering at least five women. He has since been convicted of three of those murders and is serving his sentence, life without any possibility of parole. And yet God showed me one day how deeply he loved this man who had committed such heinous crimes.

This day there were just two of us from our group at the justice center. My friend and I sat at the table, all ready for our Bible study.

A man whom we did not recognize was brought in and sat next to me and had our Bibles next to us.

Just a few minutes into this teaching, I was interrupted. I was sitting silently next to this man and listening to the teaching. I was also silently praying because my skin was crawling as I sat next to him. Interiorly, I heard these words spoken to me, *Pray a Chaplet of Divine Mercy.* I knew I heard them. The voice was entirely too clear to mistake what just had happened. I paused a moment and looked over at my friend who was still teaching and speaking. Her Bible was sitting on the table across from me. It was closed as she was teaching from a paper at this point. However, a red pamphlet was sticking out of its pages. It was the prayers of the Chaplet of Divine Mercy. I responded to the voice while saying to myself, *Lord, no one interrupts this woman while she is teaching!*

My friend is an extraordinarily holy woman. That is not a compliment, it is just an undeniable truth. She has such a commanding speaking presence. I did not want to interrupt her. Here is a good comparison to help you visualize what I mean. How many people do you think interrupted John the Baptist as he was preaching and proclaiming a baptism of repentance?

I asked Jesus if I could wait until the teaching was over. The voice in my mind interrupted again with these words, *Pray the Chaplet of Divine Mercy for him.* My heart sank. I didn't want to do it. Then I glanced over at my friend's Bible. The Chaplet of Divine Mercy pamphlet was now sitting on top of her Bible. No one had touched it, yet it had been moved out from the inner pages to the top of the Bible.

I interrupted the lesson and said we had to pray a Chaplet of Divine Mercy right away. Though stunned, my friend quietly said okay and allowed me to lead the chaplet. I pulled out my rosary beads from my pocket and put them in the hands of the man sitting so close to me that his body was right up against mine. My skin was crawling the entire time I did this. I literally held my hands over his as I showed him how to pray this particular prayer. His face was only inches from mine. My hands were over his the entire time we prayed. This man not only allowed this but he very reverently spoke each prayer. He prayed with us, "For the sake of His sorrowful Passion, have mercy on us and on the whole world. Eternal Father, I offer you the body and blood, soul and divinity, of your dearly beloved son, Our Lord Jesus Christ, in atonement for our sins...."

That did it. Part of the way through the chaplet, I could feel and hear him choke up. Something happened in his heart and soul. I could feel the struggle going on in him as he fought to stifle the tears in his chest. He continued to pray, "For the sake of his sorrowful passion..." and all the other prayers until the chaplet was finished. Seconds later, after we finished the prayer, a guard shouted out this man's name and told him he was to be transported to another part of the jail. That fast he was gone. My friend and I were frozen to our spots.

We both knew very well who this man was. We watched stories about him every night on the news. We did not recognize him because his appearance was so different from what we saw on TV. One of the woman he was accused of murdering was someone we ministered to at the justice center for many months. A few weeks after she was released, her body was found in a dumpster. The five of us in our Bible study group were heartbroken over this loss of one of God's precious children. I was sickened when I realized whom I had been sitting next to. I thought of my father. In a flash I remembered so much of the diabolical abuse I had endured. My heart ached at the terror and pain his victims must have suffered. No wonder my skin was crawling in his presence. The voice interrupted one more time and corrected me. The correction was gentle but a correction just the same. *You have no idea how he became the monster he became. I do!*

My contrition was instant and true because I think it was Jesus himself who put it there. I interiorly knew I had offended Jesus' heart. I had judged this man as soon as I knew who he was. I must tell you something else that I know hurt God's heart. Had I known who he was before the man sat down, I would not have done what Jesus asked. I would not have prayed with him. I would have made an excuse because of what was done to me. God knew that so he hid that knowledge from me.

God loves each one of us so deeply and intensely without exception. His love is not based on what we have done. It is because of who we are. We are his BELOVED, every single one of us. Even this serial killer was not outside God's extravagant mercy and love. He also was one of God's precious children. The tears choked back in this man's chest to the point that he could barely speak. I knew he felt Jesus lovingly touch his heart. I was not called to judge this man. I was only called to love him with God's love.

For the past fifteen years I have been a Kairos Prison Ministry retreat volunteer. Kairos is a Greek word that means "special time with God." The motto of this ministry is "Listen, Listen, Love, Love." I get it, Lord! You don't have to tell me twice, but I see the humor in this motto for me! I will never forget the lesson Jesus taught me when he put a serial killer in my path. Listen. Listen. Love. Love!

During these retreats, this special time with God, prisoners are lavished with love. That is what God's love does. It pours over you and through you. It ravishes your soul. This happens through all the talks, prayer services, singing, sharing activities and wonderful meals prepared by Kairos volunteers.

Here is an example of what God's agape love can do in the heart and soul of a participant during their special time with God. During the closing ceremony a woman got up to speak. Holding back tears, she went on to tell all of us that she would never get out of prison. She knew she would be there until Jesus called her home. She said this with a smile on her face and tears in her eyes. She said that no one would shut her up ever again. She was beaming when she told us that she would spend the rest of her life in prison telling anyone who would listen what she learned on her Kairos journey.

I sat there stunned once again as I listened to every word. My heart was filled with a mixture of sorrow, joy and gratitude. I knew something about this woman that I am not sure anyone else did. This same woman came up to me during a break and talked about one of the things that touched her heart so deeply. She was referring to a talk I had given that day. As she listened to me give my talk, she realized that there were others out there who had experienced similar horrors to what she had lived. She had no idea whatsoever that it was possible to forgive such heinous crimes. She had been abused in a very similar way as I had been on that kitchen table that day as a child in kindergarten.

I remember the day I wrote my talk. I did not want to share that story. It was an awful experience for me to put those words on the paper for the first time. I didn't want to do it, only I knew I was supposed to do it. God answered my prayer. He used me to help heal the wounds of another. That is the greater good that can be accomplished with all the abuse I have suffered. God can use it to bring others to him. He can love others through me. Arlene has asked me so many times during these past few years of writing together, "Elisa, please write about forgiveness. You must write about that. How were you able to forgive all that?" The answer to your question, Arlene, is Love. Once you know that you are loved by God, that changes everything! That is how I have been able to forgive. I did none of that on my own. Jesus did that in me.

It all began with LOVE.

Moments of Grace

Jesus says in John 15:9 that he loves us just as the Father loves him. Jesus tells us to remain in his love. Jesus is in you speaking these words: Just as the Father loves me ... infinitely and unconditionally ... I love you ... remain in my love ... stay there ... in my love ... don't ever leave my love for you. That is where I can heal you ... IN MY LOVE.

Remember the words at beginning of this chapter: "Fall in love with God. He's madly in love with you!"

Ask yourself, what do I believe about God's love for me? Here are some words of wisdom from Fr. Pedro Arrupe that may help you answer it.

Prayer

FALLING IN LOVE

Nothing is more practical than finding God,
that is, than falling in love
in a quite absolute, final way.

What you are in love with,
what seizes your imagination,
will affect *everything*.

It will decide what will get you
out of bed in the morning,
what you do with your evenings,
how you spend your weekends,
what you read, who you know,
what breaks your heart,
and what amazes you with joy and gratitude.

**Fall in love. Stay in love
and it will decide everything.**

Pedro Arrupe, S.J.

49

Meeting Arlene

Elisa and I met with Sister Janice and continued to build on stories of God's grace. Sister Janice then told me that she had met Arlene Finocchiaro at a meeting of the Associates of the Sisters of Saint Joseph. Arlene had shared a reflection she had written. Sister suggested I contact her. I did and asked her to write about what grace meant to her.

Elisa and I met with her at my home. When we started listening to one another, Elisa and I were completely captivated by the stories of her work with children and babies who were born blind and deaf. She read other stories that made us realize how much we need each other by God's design. We were both moved by her deep and spiritual images of God's healing grace.

Allow her to take you to a deeper level of understanding of how God moves in our lives. You will feel like you are right there to experience what God is telling you. The images that she paints before you are healing, comforting and filled with grace. She gives you the reassurance that God loves you so much and carries you through the darkness with his grace.

CHAPTER 5

EXPECT THE UNEXPECTED

The mist was all around me as I rocked in a little boat at the base of Niagara Falls. The water thundered as it fell from high above. You couldn't see where it was coming from but it flowed non-stop, delighting the onlookers huddled in their blue plastic ponchos. Everyone made the choice—to relish the experience and be submerged in the spray or to hide in the middle of the boat and stay dry.

Grace is like that loving mist of God's life ever flowing from the Father, the Son and the Holy Spirit. When we stick our neck out in the mist, it refreshes, guides, cleanses, heals and gives joy when we least expect it. The closer we get to the falls, the wetter we get. If we hold out our buckets, God will fill them to overflowing with his grace.

**God is able to make every grace abundant for you,
so that in all things, always having all you need, you
may have an abundance for every good work.
(2 Corinthians 9:8)**

Always carry an empty bucket. You never know when God will fill it up. Like the waterfall, God's grace is ever-flowing. With your

51

heart and mind open, hold out your bucket. His grace is there for the asking.

Ask and it will be given to you; seek and you will find; knock and the door will be opened to you. For everyone who asks, receives; and the one who seeks, finds; and to the one who knocks, the door will be opened.
(Matthew 7: 7–9)

And to the one who holds out her bucket, it will be filled.

Grace is there for the big events in our lives as well as the day-to-day smiles and nudges from God. The Spirit's intervention may be life-changing as St. Paul's experience on the road to Damascus (Acts 9:3–4) or a simple phone call from a friend. Moments of enlightenment come sometimes as gentle rain or as thunderbolts shaking the ground beneath our feet. I call these latter inspirations "Road to Damascus" moments—moments that knock us off our horse, changing our relationship with Jesus forever.

My transformation came with the call to intercessory prayer for others.

As a group leader in a parish Lenten spiritual renewal, I was given a study guide and assumed the role as teacher and discussion leader. The first few lessons went smoothly. Sharing with others was rewarding. I did not feel so much a responsibility to teach but to share my life experiences.

Chapter three was about our relationship with God. A small diagram presented a triangle with God at the top. At the bottom, one angle was "me" and at the other angle was "others." The lesson focused on one's relationship with God as interdependent on our relationship with others. To have a relationship with God had to be as good as one's relationships with others. Only through others could we complete the unity of the triangle.

As an only child and a striving overachiever, I balked at the idea that my relationship with God could not be attained between God and myself alone. I just couldn't see it—my relationship with God had to be as good as my relationships with others.

I prayed for understanding. Waiting, listening. How was I to truly understand this interdependent relationship? Why couldn't I take a path to God doing good for others without really being dependent on them?

With my eyes closed in the quiet of the Holy Spirit, pictures like a movie unfolded in my mind. A narrow bridge stretched from this world to heaven. It was made of narrow wooden slats held together with knotted ropes. The wooden slats were far apart and it was difficult to step from one to the next. I looked down at the slats and tried to judge where to place my step.

As I began to move, the slats became people, reaching out to me, grasping my arm and helping me to move from one to the next. Many of these people I did not know but whose faces were somewhat familiar. One was the face of a woman at the grocery store who had been in line with a difficult child. I had prayed for her. One was an older man whom I saw in a parking lot, walking in pain. I had prayed for him.

The Holy Spirit, my teacher, had provided me with the wisdom for my Lenten lesson. My relationship with God was no longer just between God and me but between God and all those who cross my path.

Unexpected and deeply personal—those chance encounters were held in the mind of God and pulled from my buried memories. My relationship with God and my way to heaven were dependent on my giving of myself in some way for the needs of others.

> ... humbly **regard others as more important than yourselves, each looking out** not for his own **interests, but [the interests] of others.**
> (Philippians 2:3–4)

God graced me with many lessons with the bridge experience. He showed me a little prayer for a stranger in passing was significant. If he remembered my little prayer and showed me how my heaven-bound journey was dependent on such little acts, he surely would shower grace on the person I prayed for.

God hears all our prayers, remembers them, and answers them in his time and in his way. The bridge moment of grace placed the seed in my mind and heart to pray for others in a more formal way. Through the mother of one of the priests at my parish, I was invited to join the diocesan healing ministry. Prayer teams met once a week before a monthly healing Mass. When people would approach for prayer, a team of three people were around them. One person lifted up their petition and then all three prayed. We witnessed the power of the Holy Spirit as strained faces softened under a waterfall of grace. You could not help leaving each service with your buckets full. I knew God was hearing our prayers.

When increased parent-caregiving at home demanded my time, I had to leave after eight years serving in the healing ministry. The reality of intercessory prayer stuck with me. I continue to pray for those God puts in my path. Sometimes I don't even know who they are. A little voice in my head or a twinge in the pit of my stomach nudges me to pray for someone.

In God's eyes, an ordinary moment becomes extraordinary. A truck driver was about to pull out in front of me. He had to stop because I had the right of way. He started pounding on his steering wheel, saying what I could only imagine. There was the pop in my head, "Pray for him." When I pass that intersection, I continue to pray for him even though that was years ago. It sometimes hits me that maybe I am the only one praying for him. That ordinary moment most of us have experienced became extraordinary through a moment of prayer.

Pulling out of a center city parking lot after a long day attending a conference, I was eager to get to the interstate and shoot home. A lady in a wheelchair was rolling herself across the street. I felt a little guilty for being impatient. Then I saw she had no feet. She went onto my prayer list.

Catholic grade school training still has me praying every time I hear a siren. I imagine there are others like myself praying all at the same time for those in that emergency. What a wonderful image to surround those needing help with the prayers of strangers. At those precious fleeting moments, you join with the mind of God for the good of those who cross your path.

Your path and mine are ever-present in the mind of God. Matthew (10:30) tells us God even numbers each hair on our head—100,000 hairs or more. He knows each by length, color and sheen. He knows when one falls out and when one grows in.

Whether you're having a bad hair day or a bad soul day, not a millisecond of time passes without God's undivided attention to your every need. Your every thought is held in the mind of God. You have no secrets from God.

> **Lord, you have probed me, you know me:**
> **you know when I sit and stand:**
> **you understand me from afar.**
> **You sift through my travels and my rest;**
> **With all my ways you are familiar.**
> **Even before a word is on my tongue, Lord, you know it all.**
> **(Psalm 139: 1–4)**

We think we are good at keeping secrets, those inner pains and doubts that we hide from those closest to us and those we just pass in our daily routines. How many times does someone ask, "How are you doing?" We answer, "Fine." What we really want to say is I am barely hanging on. This is especially true when a challenge goes on for years and there's no end in sight.

Every cell of our being cries out to God and the universe for help. We want to be like the woman who touched the fringe of Jesus' garment. We want to know he is turning to us, extending his hand to lift us up and speak the words, "Courage, daughter! Your faith has saved you." (Mt 9:22) We want an immediate healing, an end to our trial. When we ask and it doesn't come, we may question God if he really cares or even if he exists.

After more than twenty years of caring for parents and their medical needs, I was at the end of my rope. That is where a rope begins to unwind and come apart.

I was like the rope—frayed. I had grown up caring for my sick family and I should have been good at it. I had lots of practice. My parents and I lived with my uncle and my mother's parents. My mother was physically challenged from polio and my grandfather was blind from an industrial accident. Both my grandmother and grandfather were cared for at home when dying of cancer. At that time, there were no home services or hospice care. Our family pitched in and did it all.

Early in our marriage, my husband and I helped care for my husband's father. He spent his last year bedridden in a semi-coma, not able to communicate and needing full-time nursing care. He had occasional nurse visits and we had a neighbor who helped with his daily care. After his passing, my mother in-law was diagnosed with Parkinson's Disease. Slowly she lost the ability to do the things she loved. She was a wonderful Italian cook and she loved to entertain her friends and relatives. As she lost her ability to speak clearly, visitors and callers became less frequent. She was no longer safe in the kitchen and could not cook her favorite foods. To add insult to injury, she had to put up with whatever I could throw together after a busy day at work. Since we lived next door, we spent almost half our time at her house.

My parents relocated from Chicago to the East coast and moved into the house next to my mother-in-law right after my father-in-law died. My parents were welcomed by all my husband's Italian cousins. Being part of a warm family community made the relocation well worth such a big move late in life. After nine years living near us, my father passed from leukemia. Shortly after, my husband's brother died from a terminal brain tumor.

My mother, already frail from the aging effects of polio, was confined to bed with congestive heart failure. When we were not at work, we were balancing time between our mothers. A few years after my mom's passing, my mother in-law developed terminal lung cancer. Through all of this, we also dealt with health issues and six major relocations for my daughter.

Juggling multiple households, ill parents, my job, and our daughter's needs, I was sleep-deprived and overwhelmed. I hardly saw my husband who worked nights and weekends. I'd come home and we'd have the changing of the guard. During his mother's last months, he would stay through the night with her and I would go home to rest up for my work day. My husband is my gift from God, who cared for us all with calm and humor.

When my cat, my night-time companion, was killed by two roaming dogs, that was my last straw. She was a comfort and joy. My rope snapped. I saw no end to my trials. Would this cycle ever end? I needed a miracle.

I didn't ask for a miracle. I prayed but was too distraught to even think of asking for a miracle. I just wanted the daily struggle to be over.

I continued at work, putting on my happy face for the children and staff at school. I worked with handicapped children with deafness and deaf-blindness. As an occupational therapist, I was supposed to make life better for them. I saw no way of making life better for me. In hindsight, that was part of my problem—"me" and more "me." Things were beyond my control and I was too lost to give them over to God. I perceived God as with me in that vague sort of "God loves everybody" mode and I really did not give my life over to him. But when you can't dig deep enough for God, God digs deep enough for you.

One day at the coffee machine in the teachers' lounge, I reached into my pocket and grabbed some change. When I opened my hand, I could not believe my eyes. Sitting amongst the silver coins was an Indian head penny. I had never seen one before. As I explored the coin, the date read 1899. That was the year my father was born.

An overwhelming feeling of warmth and love flooded over me, as I knew and felt my father's love. I started crying and could not stop the healing tears. There I was crying and telling my friends my father loves me. Suddenly I was not alone. I felt my father, God, and all of heaven around me. I was a "fellow citizen with the holy ones and members of the household of God." (Ephesians 2:19)

Now I know pennies can come from heaven. One penny made me richer than if I were given a million bucks. That penny came from the heart of God—a heart pouring out love for me. It was an unearned gift, totally unexpected, rare, and with deep personal meaning. God knew when I read the date, a well of pain would be released from the inner depths of my heart. The penny was just a worn rare coin to everyone in that teachers' lounge. To me it was worth so much more. To me it was a sign that I was worth more. It connected me again to the love and care that my father had for me all of my life. He is still caring for me through the lifeline of the communion of saints.

The penny from heaven taught me that intercessory prayer can work both ways. We can pray for loved ones who have passed and they can pray for us. My father surely had a role in my receiving that 1899 Indian head penny.

Knowing you are supported in prayer gives you hope. When you pray for loved ones who have passed or the holy souls in purgatory that you don't even know, they are grateful and will pray for you.

The visual imagery about a mud mountain conveys my understanding of intercessory prayer. So fill up your buckets and climb with me.

Did you ever get stuck in the mud ... really stuck? I was lucky to escape a cattail mud trap on a camping trip but some of my friends did not. They had wandered off the path and got stuck up to their knees in mud and had to be dragged out. Their shoes and boots were sucked right off their feet by the heaviness pulling them down. They were lucky to have friends close by to help pull them out.

Mud is heavy and holds you down so you can't move. Mud in our lives and our spirits does the same and keeps us from moving on. We need the help of others to pull us out. Sometimes that help is through prayer.

Picture yourself at the foot of a mountain. People are climbing the mountain and some are getting stuck in the mud. You begin lugging buckets of water to wash off their mud. Slowly, those you help are released from the mud and are able to resume their climb.

Eventually, you begin to get stuck in the mud. You look ahead and see the path uphill is brighter and the path is clear. There is a bright light at the top of the mountain. You feel the mud pulling you down and you try to pull yourself up higher. But now you have mud on your arms and hands as well. When it starts to dry, it becomes stiff. Like a statue with your arms outstretched, you yearn to move on but can't. As you feel the stiffness like a cast around you, you feel frozen in mind and spirit. You can't think. You can't cry for help. You can't move. You just exist until someone acts on you.

Suddenly there is activity up ahead. The people you have helped are gathering buckets of water and pouring them down the mountainside. A gentle river and mist surrounds you, cleaning off the mud. With the gentle waves, you feel no judgment, only relief. You do not feel muddy but clean and dry. Looking to the light, you are able to continue up the path.

When we are in the mud and mire of physical, emotional and spiritual pain, intercessory prayer washes us clean. The body of Christ works to heal us, a healing we cannot achieve on our own. We don't even have to know we are being prayed for or know who is praying. I am ever so grateful when someone says they are praying for me or my family. Intercession is never wasted. It is part of that cleansing stream that frees us to move on.

No matter what is happening in your life, God is there and he is the only one who knows how you can move on. When I retired, God had a whole new list of changes for me. More transformations. I don't accept change easily and when I sense a call from him I start with doubts, rather than a resounding "Yes!" More likely, my reply is, "You want me to do *what*? I don't know how to do that." He nudges. Once I give my doubts, fears and inadequacies over to him, a sense of calm sweeps over me.

God wants us to always be changing, drawing closer to him. It means not only spending more time with him but cleaning up our act. Change immediately sets off that "Oh, no!" signal in my head. At the beginning of every school year, I walked into the "world of change"—new forms, new procedures, new standards, new federal and state regulations, and so on. I finally got the hang of it by the end of the last school year and I had to start all over. Change implies effort and a period of discomfort.

How does God get us through change? Grace, grace and more grace.

Writing is one of the challenges he set before me. I thought retirement was supposed to be an ongoing vacation. Instead, it's been back to the books. Now more than ever I am being challenged to trust in his ways. In my career as an occupational therapist, I had forty-five years of building my skills. Starting over to build new skills still has me sliding into doubts about what I can do. I have to keep reminding myself that all things are possible in God. He keeps me baited, placing stepping stones—opportunities for learning and writing companions to support me along the way.

For my thoughts are not your thoughts,
Nor are your ways my ways.
(Isaiah 55:8)

When the five of us in this book were challenged to write about how we understood God's grace and how it unfolded in our lives, a whole new spiritual journey began. The more I tuned into God and was aware of his love, the more I wanted to go deeper. I have come to expect the unexpected, moments of grace that delight, comfort and heal.

My model for dealing with the unexpected is Jesus' mother, Mary. She is the Queen of the Unexpected. A teenager betrothed but not fully married becomes pregnant through the Holy Spirit. Who saw that coming!? Well, maybe Isaiah. Then she gives birth in an animal shelter and is visited by shepherds and kings. She joyfully presents her child in the temple and is told a sword will pierce her heart. Then she has to get out of the country because the king is trying to kill her child. And this is just the beginning. Through all her trials, she accepted and didn't question the will of God.

I can't say I look forward to the "unexpected" but, when it comes, I know there's a lesson and a blessing in it somewhere. Accepting the unexpected is a big change for me. One I have to work on. I like to be in control, know the whole picture, accept change only when it is comfortable for me. At work I developed individual educational plans for students, therapy plans, consultation plans, seminar plans, power points and on and on to plan a whole year ahead and all the little steps that were needed to fulfill the plans. Now God is doing the planning and I have to listen. He gives me one step at a time. He puts me on a ladder in a fog, letting me see and climb one rung at a time. He knows with too much change at one time, I'd slide down a few rungs or fall off the ladder.

Expect to be graced in unexpected ways. Believe that God loves you. What transformed me from hearing God loves me to knowing and believing it? For me it was gifted experiences like the penny from heaven and the bridge that were unexpected and deeply personal.

God surprises. My husband's quick quips save me from many a dark and winding spiral but God's sense of humor reaches deep into my soul. When I'm really sinking, I rely on Jesus to pull me from the depths, like Peter being pulled from the raging sea. In receiving the Eucharist, I can open my heart, hold out my bucket, and be filled. I never know what he will give me but he knows better than I what I need. Once an image popped into my head of me in a hazmat suit—unexpected, right? There I was covered in a white suit, big boots and gloves and only a small slit from which to see. The suit was bulky and I wobbled around like a toddler stuffed in a snow suit. I had started my communion meditation with a burdened spirit but couldn't help laugh at myself. The message was clear—"I've got you covered." Nothing was going to get in the suit to hurt me.

I shared my image with a few friends over breakfast—a time I like to refer to as "diner" therapy. I am very fortunate to have spirit friends. These are people in my walk with Christ with whom I am able to share my spiritual journey. I was surprised that such a silly and simple image hit home with both of them. In this age of social media, a quick visual image speaks volumes and is mandatory if you want to sell anything. Well, Jesus' image did the trick. It was direct, easily shared, memorable and meaningful. Everyone got the message:

trust in him, he has you protected. You know Jesus loves you when he gives you a hazmat suit!

Be ready. Stick your neck out and hold out your bucket to receive from the waterfall of grace. God will be delighted and smile on you, giving you all that is for your good.

> **The Lord, your God, is in your midst, a mighty savior,**
> **Who will rejoice over you with gladness, and renew you**
> **in his love, Who will sing joyfully because of you....**
> **(Zephaniah 3:17)**

Moments of Grace

At the end of the day, ponder if anything unexpected has crossed your path.

Find a spirit friend with whom you can share how God has touched you personally in some way. Once you open yourself to others, they will confirm how God has worked in their lives.

Find a place of silence and read Psalm 139. Drink in the beauty of each phrase and listen to how God personally speaks to you.

Prayer

I place myself under your waterfall of grace
with open mind, heart, and hands.
I will look to the littlest things in my day
and know they are touched by your unconditional love.
So when I pick up my hairbrush and look down at those lost hairs,
I will thank you for not forgetting any of them.

CHAPTER 6

WALK INTO THE LIGHT

Imagine you cannot see. You cannot hear. You only feel the surface beneath you as you lie on your back. You do not know anything about where you are or what is going to happen to you except you know by touch that someone will care for you. This is the world of a baby born deaf and blind.

For almost thirty years I worked with children with hearing and vision impairments and multiple disabilities. Their challenges and struggles were shared by their families, caretakers and professional staff. Minor achievements were major miracles. As much as I touched them, they touched me.

Each child begins to recognize your touch just as if it were the sound of your voice. I used a specific sign-language hand shape to identify myself when I greeted each child. For one particular infant, he held his fingers fisted. I would gently open his hand and place my hand shape in his palm.

I would visit him weekly to communicate through touch and movement. Month after month I continued the greeting, opening his fingers. After three months of this routine, I touched his hand to let him know someone was there. To my surprise, he spontaneously opened his hand to allow me to place my hand-shape greeting in his palm. I was almost moved to tears. Opening his hand to mine was his acceptance—"Yes, I'm ready to play with you. I know who you are. I trust what we will do together."

Seeking a relationship with Jesus often starts like the baby who is deaf and blind. You need to be still and shut out the visual and sound distractions around you. You wait for his touch. You do not know what is going to happen to you. Your body and spirit may be tense with apprehensions of the unknown. The Lord waits for you to open your hand, your mind, your heart. Come out of your darkness and walk into his light. As with the infant, it may take many visits before you feel safe. But he is touching you always, waiting for you to say, "Yes, I'm ready. I know who you are. I trust what we will do together."

Once you experience the joy of that graced moment, the seeking begins. You look forward to your time together, whether it be in prayer or serving others. You know you are no longer alone and Jesus is just a touch away. Just open your hand.

For I am the Lord, your God, who grasp your right hand;
It is I who say to you, Do not fear, I will help you.
(Isaiah 41:13)

Total trust in God doesn't come easy for me. Giving myself to God's care has been a journey of awareness. My students taught me what total trust is all about. Many of my students did not process our concept of God intellectually, but they experienced his love and care through the actions of family and caregivers. Some had significant health issues requiring 24-hour nursing care. They were dependent on others for every daily need.

I was overwhelmed by the thought of being dependent on others for everything, including clearing my airway to breathe—all day, every day. Even in their dependent state, the children were always giving to me—a smile, a touch, an intellectual or physical challenge. If they did not see the world, how could I bring it to them? If they did not hear, how could I communicate to them? If we are not seeing

Jesus or listening to his voice, he still finds ways to touch us and bring us into his light. He is with us to give us strength to see the things he wants us to see and hear the things he wants us to hear. The Spirit most often speaks to us in a quiet gentle breeze—in the small things. Just keep your eyes and ears open. You never know when God is going to put a message in your path.

When I was walking through a local park, I spotted a group of pine needles washed onto the road in the early morning rain. They were in the shape of a perfect heart. I knew that heart was there for me. It would be gone later in the day. To me it was a little love note from God for me to notice along my way. Look for those little moments of grace in your day.

No matter who we encounter during the day, we are giving something of ourselves to the other person and they are giving to us. Jesus wants us to give him to others and for us to accept him from others. How often do we need the loving touch of others to get through our day? Others can touch your heart in ways you least expect.

One of my young students with deaf-blindness was medically fragile and required 24-hour nursing care. He could hear some sound and see some light. When I'd visit, I'd present stories with sensory experiences—things to touch, colored lights, and gentle movements of his arms. He liked a story about a mother and baby polar bears. Two fuzzy bears accompanied the book and I touched the fuzzy bears to his cheeks and his hands. I fanned the cool breezes of the North Pole on the side of his face and he smiled. He bravely accepted new challenges to his senses with each new story adventure. What trust he had when I introduced things to touch that he did not see or understand by any verbal explanation. This was a shining example of the child-like trust Jesus wants us to have and be open to what he sends our way.

I had worked with this student and his family since he was six months old. Now at age five, he was dying.

When I arrived at his home for what would be my last visit, he had been unresponsive to the efforts of his caregivers. I tried our favorite story with the polar bears but there was no familiar head turn or smile. I just held his hand and talked with his nurse for some time. Before I left, I gave him a kiss on the forehead, told him I loved him and made my prayerful goodbye. At that moment, he let out a noticeable sigh. For me, that was his goodbye. He could no longer give anything but a sigh.

At his funeral Mass, I pondered on what he would do in heaven. A picture came to mind of him running happily—just running and more running. In life he could barely move. He was now whole and enjoying the wide open spaces of heaven.

Weeks later, I relayed the running story to his mom. To my surprise, she told me that his three-year-old brother had seen him running through their house.

This was a precious gift to me—a confirmation that the picture I saw of him running was not just my imagination. There was the grace of consolation that not only enveloped me for his passing, but for two other precious little students of mine that passed the same school year. In God's love they were being all that God wanted them to be.

My student's life was a gift to us all, teaching us about the smallest efforts in life and their value. Even from heaven, he was letting us know that what is best for us is still to come.

I wrote to his family that in many ways he was my teacher.

From the beginning, he was always teaching;

Teaching me of love, openness of spirit, and perseverance.

Teaching me to look for and share the smallest and most personal things in life,

A touch, a breath, a sigh, a whimper, a smile, a tear.

Teaching me that together we are better than we are alone.

A warm hand was always ready to try new things,
A spirit for adventure to touch, to move into the unknown.
Teaching all, that gentleness of heart
Is a greater achievement than climbing the highest mountain.

To help teachers better understand the sensory losses of our students, I worked with a team of educational specialists to provide in-service training. The participants wore blindfolds and ear plugs to simulate loss of vision and hearing during simple daily tasks.

When I had experienced the simulation activities myself, it gave me an awareness of being thrust into darkness and silence. My guide took my hand, signaling me to stand. There was no talking, only communication by touch. She placed my left hand on her right arm above her elbow. In this position, she was my sighted guide and could lead me in any direction. I felt her pace when it was safe to walk. I turned as she turned. I paused as she paused. If there was a change from sidewalk to grass, she slowed so I could adjust. Total trust was placed in her for my safety. Then she came to a stop. She took my hand to touch a chair and signaled for me to sit. Then she left. My lifeline was gone. I was totally abandoned to nothingness except my inner fears. Where was I? What was going to happen to me? How long would I be there?

If I decided to get up and wander around on my own, all types of dangers awaited. When my guide finally touched my hand, I felt saved. My perception of time in the darkness was distorted. I thought I had been left for fifteen or twenty minutes when it was only five.

How often do we let go of Jesus' hand and flounder around on our own? He is our sighted guide—the truth and the light. When we let go, we are in darkness. When we hold on and let him lead, he keeps us on the right path. His hand is always there. Don't let go.

**Trust in the Lord with all your heart, on
your own intelligence do not rely;**

In all your ways be mindful of him, and
he will make straight your paths.
(Proverbs 3:5–6)

The hardest part of that proverb for me is "on your own intelligence do not rely." For "miss wanting to be in control," there is a constant struggle between the "I want" and "God wants." I spent most of my life acquiring skills for my career to be the best I knew how to be. And, yes, that is from the Army motto. I started my career as an officer in the Army during the Vietnam war. So "Be all that you can be" is still lurking in my mind. But now Jesus speaks to my heart, *be all that I want you to be.* John the Baptist said it best:

He must increase; I must decrease.
(John 3:30)

Little did I know as a child with a grandfather who was blind that God would set my career path working with children with deaf-blindness.

My memories of my grandfather take me to our basement in a Chicago bungalow. My grandfather tended the furnace to warm us through the cold Chicago winters. I loved to watch him open the boiler door and shovel coals into the fiery blast. The glow and heat were scary to me. I stood far away and marveled how he managed safely without seeing. Before he lost his sight, he had worked in the coal mines as a child. The smell of coal must have been in his blood.

Grandfather would sing to me and push me on a little homemade swing hung from the basement beams. He was a gentle, quiet man with a soft spot for his granddaughter. If I close my eyes and listen to my heart, his song comes back about the streets of New York.

One of my weekly duties as a child was running errands to the store a few blocks away from home. I'd walk guiding my grandfather, holding his hand. We'd stop at the bakery, the butcher, the grocery and sometimes the pharmacy. I held his hand and he held the cash.

On the way home, we'd stop at the tavern where he'd have a beer and talk with friends. He gave me pennies for the peanut machine—a bribe to keep me quiet about the tavern stop. Eventually, grandmother found out and that was the end of the peanuts.

Grandfather spent most of his days sitting in an old cushioned rocker, listening to the radio. Sometimes I would climb on his lap and we'd rock together. As I got older, I became distracted with other interests and spent little time attending to him. Working with individuals with sensory impairments taught me the isolation he must have experienced as I had with my sighted guide simulation.

God has lovingly brought me through life gifting me with being a light for my grandfather and my students with sensory impairments.

For those of us gifted with sight, how do we use it towards our heavenly goal? Do we look into the face of Jesus? Do we see how much he loves us? Do we see Jesus in others? Do we see the opportunities he places before us?

Jesus brought his light curing individuals with deafness or blindness. The story of the blind man from Bethsaida in Mark's gospel (8:22–26) holds many lessons for me. First, his friends begged Jesus to touch him. So often we ask our friends to pray for us, beg Jesus to help us. They knew Jesus' touch or just touching Jesus would cure their friend. Jesus promised to answer prayer if two or more make the request. Even if each of your friends prays one tiny little prayer, they all add up.

So many people reached out to Jesus for healing. He had recently fed 4,000 with bread and fish and I'm sure those 4,000 told 4,000 more (Mark 8:1–9). Crowds followed him everywhere.

For the blind man, Jesus sought privacy. Jesus took him by the hand and led him outside the village, away from crowds. How often does Jesus want our healing to be in private? Does he pull you away from your routine—take you aside?

Jesus then gave of himself, spitting on the blind man's eyes and laying on his hands. He didn't say, "You are cured" or "Your sins are forgiven," as he said with others. Jesus asked, "Do you see anything?" Jesus must have been reaching for more than sight from this man's heart. Did the man have the faith to see physically and spiritually?

The man responded—and this is what blows my mind—"I see men, but they look like trees, walking." Since I had been steeped in eight years of intensive training to assess and intervene for children with cortical visual impairment, I knew what the man was seeing. His eyes took in light but his brain could not identify what was really in front of him. In other cures in the gospels, the blind men just went happily on their way.

Jesus again laid his hands on the man's eyes. Healing did not happen all at once. We know Jesus could do it. He had so much to teach us here. I know, for me, healing often comes in stages. Some issues take years and Jesus asks, "Do you see anything? Do you see how I am working in your life? Are you ready for more healing?"

After the man was cured, Jesus told him to go home and not to enter the village. For this man, I think Jesus wanted him to linger in quiet and not be thrown into village crowds, pressing in on him and questioning him about his healing. I think there was more than the healing of his vision that was to be ongoing. Sometimes I have to go to a quiet place to rest and heal.

A blind man in Jesus' time was considered a sinner, a beggar or one to be shunned or pitied. I don't know for sure about this particular man but I can be sure that after he was cured he had to take on a new identity, a new role in his family and his community. That would take some time. As with those he cured in the gospels, Jesus was sensitive not only to what a person endured prior to healing but was sensitive to how one deals with healing and what occurs after it. He stays by our side to continue any further healing that is needed.

The man in the gospel was used to being led. When Jesus sent him home, he had the awesome ability for his brain to process the visual information to know where to go. All of the years of neuronal brain development to get to that stage of visual knowledge occurred in an instant. Seeing was not just having his eyes work. Seeing was knowing—his whole brain and body worked as if they had been working together since his birth.

The man cured of his blindness had a whole new way to interact with his world. For him normal had been not seeing. He knew he was missing something but not sure of what it really was. When Jesus lifted his hands from the man's eyes a second time, Jesus' face was the first thing he saw. He had never looked upon anyone's face until Jesus. What did he look at first? His eyes? His beard? Did he see in Jesus' face how much Jesus loved him? Was he able to gaze into Jesus' eyes with his own and express his joy? How joyful we can be when we receive Jesus in the Eucharist and he is held up before our eyes!

Because of Jesus, this man now walked in the light. With his vision restored, how was he going to use it? Was he going to help others? Was he going to repay any kindness of those who had supported him? Was he going to remember the love shining from the face of Jesus? How was he going to use his new-found sight?

I will lead the blind on a way they do not know; by paths they do not know I will guide them. I will turn their darkness into light before them and make crooked ways straight. These are my promises: I made them, I will not forsake them. (Isaiah 42:16)

When Jesus gifts you with his light, you want to share it. I like to picture that the five of us writing this book are shouting from the rooftops that God loves us. There are sirens and news crews scurrying about and TV cameras recording our crazy antics. They are all wondering what we are shouting. Why are we jumping about and waving our arms? Why do we want everyone to see and hear us? "God loves us!"

> **That's our message. God is the light of our lives.**
> **He is the light for everyone. Our culture has been**
> **plunged into darkness and we need all the lights we**
> **can get. Every little light gives hope to the world.**
> **No one who lights a lamp hides it away or**
> **places it [under a bushel basket],**
> **but on a lamp stand so that those who enter might see the light.**
> **(Luke 11:33)**

When God lights our lamp, we will never know how many paths have been brightened. My mom contracted polio at age two and was physically disabled her whole life. In her last few years she was confined to bed with congestive heart failure. That didn't stop her from bringing her light to others.

She kept in touch with over 300 pen pals around the U.S. and Canada, many in nursing homes. She lifted the spirits of many who were lonely. Sometimes mom's letters and cards were the only ones they received. She was limited in motion but not in spirit. I marveled at my mom's close friendships with so many people even though she was confined to bed. I have a few close friends and lots of acquaintances—but not 300.

Mom lived in the era before e-mail and I often wonder how many more friends she would have had if she had accessed the internet and social media.

Of the old school, mom hand-penned eight-page letters. She and her friends shared details of their lives down to the multi-course dinners on special occasions. Even though many facts were shared, her message was filled with words specially chosen for each one. She balked every time I suggested sending copies of letters to multiple friends.

She loved hand-decorating letters and cards. Valentines were ever-so-special when made by my mom. She made all her valentines with love for our family and her hundreds of pen pals. When she passed, her bed was strewn with pink and red hearts ready to be assembled for valentines.

Just as a message was specially chosen for each of mom's friends, the Lord does that for each one of us. When we hear the gospels, we hear the same words. The Spirit reads our hearts and the Lord individualizes his message to us. He sends his valentines, touching our minds and hearts in many ways.

I was distraught as my mom passed suddenly when I was out of town. There was little time to grieve as my husband and I had also been taking care of his mom. I was so torn in my heart that I was not there for her. Jesus later gave me peace, letting me know she was not alone. He was there.

Trusting that the Lord knows what is best for us is a mystery to which we are often blind. He gives us his gift of grace all tied up in bright paper and bows and we can only guess what's inside. It has been chosen especially for us. We can't see it. But it gives us new perspective with God's eyes. We can't hear it. But it allows us to hear what God wants us to hear. We can't touch it. But our hands become empowered to touch others. It can move us to action when our own efforts cannot overcome our inertia.

When you are blessed with a moment of light, the Spirit provides snippets of wisdom, little pearls you can add to your necklace of faith, like those beads you add to a necklace in remembrance of special occasions.

To walk into his light is to walk through this world and prepare for the next—heaven. When Jesus heals, it is for us to become stronger to get there. When he comforts, it is for us to be grateful. After Jesus cured the man at Bethsaida of blindness, his burden was lifted and he went off to start life renewed. He had to give up his old ways of living, begging and taking people's leftovers.

God does not want us to have leftovers. He wants us at his banquet, the Eucharistic feast. But that means we have to put on our best. We have to change out of our dusty and raggedy selves. This change means forgiving others as well as ourselves. Whether the pain is day after day or a one-time event, it has to be passed from our hands to Jesus and his Holy Mother to soothe the anguish in our hearts. The sacrament of Penance showers our souls reaching all the grimy spots that are hard to reach.

For those who tend to feel uncomfortable with unburdening their inner most pains, Jesus knows what they are and only wants you to bring them to him. Picture yourself cleaning out the closet of your soul. So grab an empty box and start filling it up. Jesus is ready to collect all your old junk.

Picture a large white truck pulls up to the curbside. Across the side of the truck is written "The Holy Spirit Trucking Company." A young man with a beard jumps out and opens wide the back doors. A line forms with everyone holding armfuls of old clothes, broken chairs and just plain old junk.

The young man smiles and warmly looks into each person's eyes as he lifts the weight from their arms. He loads the truck as the next person steps up in line. There is relief on each face as what was old and broken is taken from their hands.

You step up to the front of the line with a heavy box that weighs you down. You feel the strain in your back and pain in your shoulders. Your brow furrows and your eyes cast down.

The young man reaches out his arms to receive the box. You stand frozen. You have carried this box for a very long time. It is part of you. You are not sure you want to give it up. The young man tilts his head to look into your eyes and distracts your downward gaze.

With a quiet voice, he says, "Let it go." You slowly hand over the heavy box. You are embarrassed to bring your burdens to the Lord and then not hand them over.

Letting go is not easy. We become comfortable holding onto our junk—worn emotions, longstanding resentments, embers of anger, broken feelings and shreds of self-pity. The junk piles up in the back of the closets of our inner being and we forget it's there.

When we try to clean it out, the memories stir up dust and the pains are renewed. The Lord wants to take these painful moments of our lives and load them into his truck, shut the doors and drive away. All he asks is, "Let it go."

What can you clean out of the closet of your heart?

Now that we are all cleaned up, we have our eyes set on the path to the pearly gates. Are they really made of pearls? Revelation tells us, "The twelve gates were twelve pearls, each of the gates made from a single pearl...." (Revelation 21:21)

Of all the gemstones described in heaven, the pearl is the only one formed within a living creature. We know how pearls are formed within the walls of a shell. An irritant inside the shell becomes coated with layer upon layer of a pearl essence so it becomes smooth and shiny like the inside of the shell. The more layers, the more value.

Matthew 13:45–46 tells us "the Kingdom of heaven is like a merchant searching for fine pearls. When he finds a pearl of great price, he goes and sells all that he has and buys it." Jesus is our merchant who gave all he had to purchase the pearl within each one of us. That pearl can only form through his grace working within us.

What happens to irritants inside our shell? To become precious and valuable, our challenges, faults and struggles need to be coated over and over again in the light and saving grace of Jesus. Our very faults, challenges and struggles become the seeds requiring us to seek God's grace. Without these human problems there is just an empty shell with no opportunity to interact with God's grace. The more we interact with prayer and the sacraments, the more smooth pearly essence builds up on our pearl.

Each of us has a pearl growing within us. It is a mystery. We don't know its color, shape or how many bumps need to be smoothed. We only hope that someday we will present our pearl to Jesus to become part of the heavenly kingdom.

Moments of Grace

Jesus is seeing what you are seeing. He is hearing what you are hearing. Is it what you want him to see and hear?

Jesus wants you on the path to heaven. Ask him for help how to get there. Place a post-it as a reminder that it is your travel destination.

Think of how you could bring a light and a joyous sound to someone in need.

Prayer

Lord, grant me the grace to see what you want me to see,
to hear what you want me to hear.
To others, let my hands be your hands. Let my face be your face.
Let my light be your light.

Meeting Sister Janice

I met Sister Janice at a teacher workshop. She was speaking on the lives of the saints. I could barely move since she is one of the best storytellers of all time. The saints are ordinary people who had an extraordinary love for God. Although Sister Janice has her own struggles with rheumatoid arthritis, her condition does not hold her back from doing God's work.

She is a fierce advocate for people with disabilities, the marginalized, the unloved and any whom the world considers having little worth.

Sister Janice will share her life-changing spiritual experience from Lourdes, France. Listen as God speaks to you through her story. Even though your prayers may not be answered in the way you expect, God will give you the grace you need.

CHAPTER 7

GRACE: GOD'S COMMUNICATION
LOURDES, 1988

*P*eople told me it would be wonderful. I doubted them, never expecting the profound graces and spiritual lavishness of my week at Lourdes.

I was thirty-eight years old, a Sister of St. Joseph, and worked in disability ministry for the Metuchen Diocese of central New Jersey. Also, I had been diagnosed with rheumatoid arthritis twenty years before.

Paul Russell, my friend from the diocesan disability ministry, was a quadriplegic with a profound spirituality. Paul was intent on having me accompany him and his fellow Dominicans on their annual pilgrimage to Lourdes. He was so keen on my going that he even raised the funds.

Five days before we were to leave, Paul died. His body had grown weaker over the years of living with quadriplegia. His death left me in profound grief and distress. The whole trip was his idea and now he would not even be there. I no longer wanted to go. However, Paul's friends convinced me that it would be what he wanted.

Seven hours after taking off from Newark International, our group of pilgrims debarked from the plane. Although I was quite capable of walking, Paul had convinced me to use a wheelchair for the vast distances of Lourdes. The woman pushing my wheelchair asked if I would like to see the grotto, the exact spot where Mary appeared to the illiterate peasant girl Bernadette Soubrious in 1858. It was 11 p.m. French time and I was exhausted, but I also wanted to see the sacred spot that many consider the heart of Catholicism.

I believe that grace is God's way of "talking" to us, inviting us to grow. An image I have long had portrays God as knocking on the "windows" of our soul, trying to communicate with us, to gently nudge us in a good direction. I am happy that God "nudged" me into the grotto upon my arrival at Lourdes because it was there that I had the first religious experience of my pilgrimage.

As I was wheeled into the grotto, waves of transcendent awe flowed over me. It seemed as though spiritual radar emanated from the rocks that comprised the walls. I sensed, rather than thought, that what I was experiencing so profoundly came from a deep sense of the faith of the millions of pilgrims who had prayed at the grotto through the decades, running their fingers over the walls of rock while murmuring their "Aves."

While I did not know anyone in my tour group, there was a great sense of camaraderie among us. Our days consisted of trips to the grotto, Mass in French in the elegant Cathedral of Lourdes, and visiting its shops. Every evening we gathered for a parade, singing "Aves" in honor of Mary. All the while, I knew something was happening in my soul. Despite the ever-present fatigue that accompanies rheumatoid arthritis, I only slept for a few hours a night, being kept awake by a spiritual electricity continually coursing through my soul. This spiritual energy graced me with physical energy.

Unbeknownst to me, God was gently tilling the soil of my soul with this spiritual electricity, suffusing it with grace I would soon need.

For, of course, I wanted to be cured. We all wanted to be cured. We wanted to be dipped in Lourdes' famed healing waters and come out whole, restored. I waited until the end of the week. I declined all companionship, knowing that this was something I had to do alone.

As I waited in line outside the baths, with prayers and spiritual admonitions coming over the loudspeaker in several different languages, I prayed. It would be nice to say that I prayed freely, offering my fiat with Mary "Though I do not understand, God will be with me...." But I didn't. I prayed fiercely to rid my body of the inflammatory process that was robbing it of its function and capabilities. I wanted my physical strength back. I wanted to be the helper, not the helped.

The female attendant assisted me into a scanty white robe. Two women then gently lowered me into the bath itself. I was shocked at how cold the water was. I let it swirl around my body for a few moments, praying, hoping earnestly for my own private miracle.

Nothing happened. I knew immediately that I was not cured. Indeed my joints were rather vigorously protesting this unexpected frigid shock treatment. The women assisted me out of the bath, I returned to my wheelchair and pushed out into the sunlit grotto area.

Thoughts besieged my brain as feelings barraged my heart. I wasn't cured, so what? Plenty of people weren't. Many people lived with far worse than I did but a lot more lived with far less. Indeed, many with no physical concerns at all. Yes, I had coped with living with a chronic condition for 12 years, but who knew what was going to happen? Where would it attack next?

Darkness, disappointment, despair—feelings not consistent with the stellar shrine of faith before which I sat. Starting to come out of this wrenching inward self-focus, I began to look about me at my fellow pilgrims to Lourdes. I sat wheelchair ensconced, in the midst of the sea of wheelchair users, most of whom probably would be dependent on them for life, whereas I was only using mine to conserve energy around the huge grotto area.

Deep within me, in that sacred place reserved for God, I heard a consoling voice: "See, look around you. These are my people. I am with them as I am with you. I weep with them ... I cheer them on." Then again: "These are my people. And you are to speak for them."

The ground did not open up. Thunderbolts were not hurled from above. The people around me smiled and chatted as I looked at my hands, the hands I had profoundly hoped would return to their former strength and beauty. They were unchanged—shorter fingers, scars at the wrists and thumbs. But they were mine. They still got me through every day.

And now they had a mission. I knew instantly what that mission was—to become an advocate for people with disabilities both within and outside the church. To join the national effort for disability civil rights. To become a bridge-builder between the disability community and the church. To do this for and with the One who weeps for His people.

No, I did not receive the grace I so eagerly sought from my pilgrimage to Lourdes. I was not cured.

I was anointed.

As God makes clear "... my thoughts are not your thoughts, nor are your ways my ways...." (Isaiah 55:8) When I went to Lourdes in 1987, I knew exactly what grace *I* desired. I wanted to be hale and hearty—to have the inflammatory process that was tearing at my joints stop completely. That didn't happen. Instead, I received a greater grace: I was clear about who I was now, a woman religious with a disability. I was also clear about what I was to do. I had been working in disability ministry within the church already, but now I knew that God wanted me to speak and advocate for acceptance, accessibility, and, most difficult of all, attitudinal change toward people with disabilities.

I went back to my job in the Diocese of Metuchen, New Jersey, with a renewed spirit.

After Barbara asked us to write about how we bring Jesus to others, I reflected about my attempts to do just that through my life as a Sister of St. Joseph, my ministry for years with people with all kinds of disabilities, and writing two books about saints from a disability perspective.

Initially, I struggled with my call to become a religious. After I explained this to the Vocation Director of the Sisters of St. Joseph, assuring her that God would not want a flawed person like me, she brushed away my arguments, saying I was not too old at 30 and that God calls us with our flaws as well as our gifts. She also told me to pray and listen with my heart to what God was saying. So I did. After a year of praying and discerning, I left my teaching job, gave my cat to my mother, my car to my sister and entered the Postulate of the Sisters of St. Joseph in 1983. I have loved living with other sisters, centering our lives around prayer and the sacraments.

At that point, I was eager to follow Jesus myself, but I was not consciously thinking about bringing Jesus to others. However, as a Sister of St. Joseph, I try to connect people with God as often as I can. I consider myself fortunate to live a lifestyle that has God as the center of my life and I try to share the importance of having God in their life with others.

It is for this reason that I chose to study spirituality/spiritual direction at Chestnut Hill College. I wanted to do my best to share the goodness of God with others. I believe that there is a deep spiritual thirst among people today. Many make the mistake of not realizing that God is with them *always*, not just in church. We are to follow at all times the example of Jesus, who treated others with love and mercy, stressed the importance of caring for people who were poor and marginalized and, most of all, taught us the importance of prayer.

When I am in a direction session with someone, I am aware what a tremendous privilege it is to accompany people on their life's journey with God. Being a spiritual director has taught me how to listen differently. It took me a while to stop going to my head and trying to fix things for people. Instead, I do my best to listen contemplatively and follow the inner promptings of the spirit. I just try to get out of the way and do my best to have my directee focus on God.

Most people genuinely want to do God's will, particularly in major life decisions. This usually requires discernment as to exactly what God's will is for them. After intense prayer to the Spirit, we try to prayerfully go over the pros and cons of a decision. Any decision or course of action that is genuinely of God brings peace, inner harmony, and calm.

As I had spent my youth and my early adulthood without a disability, I could empathize with people who were newly disabled from an accident or illness. I was also able to relate to anyone who had lived with a disability long-term. Due to my own journey, I knew how important it was to bring Jesus to these Diocesan parishioners with disabilities. With the help of parish ministers, we organized support/ prayer groups for disabled people and their parish and their families and friends. Aware of the rejection that can accompany life with a disability, I tried to stress again and again that Jesus was with us in our struggles, as he promised in the end of Matthew's Gospel: "... I am with you always, until the end of the world!" (Matthew 28:20)

With the support of Bishop Edward Hughes, I held diocesan-wide retreat days for people with disabilities. This was an opportunity for people to get to know one another and also receive spiritual sustenance, which is crucial when living with a disability. We ended the day with Mass celebrated by Bishop Hughes, who always told us jokingly that his disability was his bald head!

Again from my own life, I was aware of how isolating disability can be for a person. I was still able to drive at that time and I would visit as many disabled parishioners as I could. I remember one thirty-year-old woman who had had a stroke while she was pregnant with her little girl. Fortunately, her daughter was delivered safely, but she was left with little ability to speak. This is an extremely difficult disability, as she told me how often people hung up on her when she called because it took her so long to get her words out.

The flip side of my ministry was raising awareness about disability. At that time, the late 1980s, the Americans with Disabilities Act had not been passed and there was little outreach of any kind to disabled people. I organized Disability Awareness Liturgies in parishes, which involved having parishioners with various disabilities serve in different roles during a regular Sunday Mass. Sometimes I would have a blind person lector (this has tremendous witness value), a person in a wheelchair distribute communion, and individuals with intellectual disabilities serve as greeters and ushers. Generally, I would speak after Communion and invite the congregation to follow the example of Jesus, who constantly reached out to people who were blind, had leprosy, or were unable to walk. I tried to stress that it is human to be afraid of disability, but to ask Jesus for the grace to replace that fear with faith, the faith that he will always be with us.

Finally, I felt called to bring Jesus to others through writing. God gifted me with the ability to write and speak and I wanted to use these gifts as best I could for his people. Also, I was keenly aware of the spiritual thirst among all people, but particularly among disabled people. Part of the reason I decided to study spirituality was to connect people to God.

After writing a paper for a spirituality course about how Saint Therese of Lisieux, the Little Flower, coped spiritually with her terminal illness of tuberculosis, I felt invited by God's Spirit to write about other saints with disabilities or illnesses. I felt it would help disabled individuals to have role models, to know that someone among the communion of saints also lived with physical suffering and emotional pain.

My hope was to lift the lens of disability to the lives of various members of the communion of saints to see how they could help us today. Cardinal Joseph Bernadine of Chicago, who was diagnosed with pancreatic cancer, has much to teach us about letting go and surrendering to God. The story of Venerable Matt Talbot, who battled alcoholism, offers hope not only for people with addictions, but also their families. St. Ignatius of Loyola's conversion, his Spiritual Exercises and founding of the Jesuits, all flowed from his convalescence from a war wound. His life illustrates once again how God can bring great good from any situation.

St. Anthony Messenger Press published my book in 2006 under the title *Saints to Lean On: Spiritual Companions for Illness and Disability.* After it was published, I began to be invited to give presentations and days of reflection to parish groups. I enjoy presenting the lives of members of the communion of saints to show that we are not alone in our struggles in life.

St. Anthony Messenger Press was pleased with the success of *Saints to Lean On* and asked me to write a second book about saints. This time my focus was on saints as healers. Some provided physical healing to others. For example, St. Damien of Molokai ministered with people with leprosy, Saint Catherine of Siena went about her city nursing people who were ill, and St. Hildegard of Bingen was well-versed in using different herbs to heal people.

However, I also wanted to look at healing in a broader way. So I chose St. Joan of Arc because her presence on the battlefield healed the morale of the soldiers of France. I was extremely impressed with Venerable Henriette DeLille, who risked imprisonment to teach slave children how to read in 19th century New Orleans. I concluded the book with Father Mychal Judge of 9/11 fame, who not only rushed into the World Trade Center to save people but also ministered with people with AIDS when no one else would touch them.

Just as I did my best to bring Jesus to other people, I was also able to see Jesus in them. I could recognize Jesus in the Garden of Gethsemane when I was with directees who agonized about their children with addictions. I saw the passion of Christ lived out again and again with people in my ministry who were quadriplegic or blind.

Occasionally after giving a presentation on one of my saints' books, I heard the heartache of Mary from mothers whose children were very ill or disabled.

We all know that life can be hard. It can include illness, disability, addiction or deep grieving for a loved one. But we must always remember that Jesus is with us in our struggles. I do my best to bring Jesus, his presence, consolation and strength to anyone who lives in any way with the sufferings of the human condition.

Moments of Grace

According to St. Paul, God's grace is sufficient for us. While I was not healed of rheumatoid arthritis at Lourdes, the profound religious experience I was given became a foundational grace for my life.

It is easy to love God when all is going well. It is more difficult when our lives are not going the way we would like. Do you have the fortitude to remain in God's love even when times are difficult?

Prayer

O God of surprises,
help me to know that a grace not given
is not a grace denied,
but rather an invitation
to ever-deepening trust in you.

Meeting Annette

I met Annette at St. Agnes Day Room where people come for prayer, food and comfort. She and I shared our desire to write about God and the rest is history. God took over from there.

Initially, Annette will take you on a journey to see God through her eyes as an innocent child.

You will experience along with her a tragedy that turned her closer to God.

She will share with you amazing stories of faith. When you accept God's grace, it will not mean that things are going to go smoothly or that you will always get what you want. It takes time to recognize and cultivate what God is doing in your life. Sometimes your world is turned upside down. Oftentimes we don't discover the goodness until much later in life. God is working. Tragedies become blessings.

With grace comes mercy. We are all in need of mercy and Annette will inspire you with her own insights to the workings of God's mercy.

CHAPTER 8

CHILDHOOD INNOCENCE

*G*race—what is grace? Is it an intellectual exercise defined in religious books? Can its meaning only be found in the Christian teachings of a theology class? Is it an outdated relic of the past?

Despite the death that grace has been dealt by the world, it is alive and well for anyone who wishes to encounter it. All around us, it is an ever-present goodness of which we are often unaware. Even though grace is found in the beauty we encounter every day, we don't point and proclaim, "There it is, that is grace."

My hope is to convey a clear understanding of grace through my own personal experiences and how I saw grace unfold in my life—to share the awareness of grace as beautiful, real and concrete. I have come to know grace not just as something we experience but as an encounter with someone.

Seeking to answer what grace is, my favorite Catholic author, Flannery O'Connor, teaches, "All human nature vigorously resists grace because grace changes us and change is painful." We humans spend our lifetime resisting change and change, when it involves our behavior, whether it be good or bad, is painful. Most often, we are dragged kicking and screaming into change.

Grace is vague and ambiguous and I have stumbled through life with a meager grasp of grace or its presence. When I look back and reflect, I see I have been tenderly shepherded through life. It is simply "God's gift" to us—a gift from heaven of his gratuitous love and mercy. By sharing some of my own experiences, you may reflect back and recognize God's love for you and develop a truly intimate relationship with him.

"Where did I come from?" I asked my mother in a panic. Her response was simple and serene, "You came from God. He sent you to us." She never stopped what she was doing and never batted an eye. She proclaimed it as simply as that. All I could say in the face of such certainty was "Oh." In my mind, it must be so. Why hadn't I thought of it myself? To a five-year-old, the answer was sufficient. It somehow clarified that I had been sent deliberately and there was so mistake. I did not just fall from the sky. My mother knew without a doubt that I had been given to her for a purpose.

This was my first memory of encountering God's grace. I have never forgotten this wonderful moment. I classify this beautiful memory as a gift of retrospective grace. Many times, I draw on this encounter to help my own children recognize his voice.

Looking back, I can hear his voice, whispering, revealing, and challenging me. When a little memory surfaces, I reflect on it and the more profound it becomes.

I was in the fourth grade, lining up for lunch. The girl in front of me was having a discussion with another girl about what God looks like. As I listened in, I was curious to know why the one girl was so perplexed about what God looks like. After all, don't we all know what he looks like? I had pictures in my home of what he looks like. The image of the Sacred Heart above my front door as you first walk into my house popped into my head. There were crucifixes in every room of my house and holy pictures permeated my parents' home. Why she was so puzzled about God's looks did not seem right and her confusion over the whole matter appeared more confounding than her actual question.

So I took it upon myself to enter the discussion and asked my classmate why she was even inquiring about such an obvious mystery. Her answer revealed much about her but much more about me. She turned around, angry that I butted into her discussion, and spat her response.

She said, "I am talking about God."

Again, I said, "Yes, yes. I know. Don't you have any pictures of him in your home?"

Much to my amazement, the girl became furious. I was simply asking a question that seemed natural. In my innocence, I thought she just lacked a simple picture of Jesus. I would have brought her a holy card if she wanted to see him. We always had handfuls at our house and I was certain my mother wouldn't mind me sharing one with this friend who didn't even know what God looked like. It was the least I could do for the poor girl. It was so clear in my mind. Not so with this young lady. She was determined to pound it into my thick skull.

With her eyes blazing and her face as red as a tomato, she screamed, "God the Father, you idiot! Don't you know who God is?"

Persistent in my ignorance, or perhaps in my comic wisdom, I said yet again, "Of course I know him. But it is apparent that you do not."

That ended the conversation.

Looking back, it was all so hilarious and, to this day, makes me laugh out loud. God is so funny—he even takes our innocence and ignorance and turns them into something grand.

The truth of the matter is, this is an Incarnation question. It is one of the three mysteries of our faith and deserves more than just a mere mention. The Incarnation is God made flesh. He took on human nature in the form of flesh, the flesh of man in all its beauty and weaknesses, in order to become one with us. The most beautiful part of all of it is he did not come with fanfare and celebration. No trumpets or royal courts present. No pomp or circumstance. None. He came alone, to a young girl in a small room accompanied only by an angel. He entered the world in humble surroundings with no prepared comforts, vulnerable to the elements, and enemies pursuing from the very beginning. Breaking through a broken world as a tiny human baby, he, the eternal Word, became flesh and dwelt among us. (John 1:14)

I could fill an entire book with wonderful examples of God's mercy and love for me. As with all of life, hardships are a measure for everybody, and I've had my share of them. My father was an alcoholic and my childhood reflects a great deal of covering up for my family's sins. I saw the difficulties that come with a less-than-perfect household. My mother was often brought to tears by the circumstances she endured. She was the rock in our family and the constant example of a saint. I do not doubt for a second that my mother sits among the communion of saints in heaven. She was the family anchor and I attribute all of my faith to her firm and consistent guidance.

I grew up rather poor but never knew or was aware of my poverty by anything my mother said or conveyed. I only became slightly aware of the fact we had a little less room in our house compared to others because I could never ask any of my friends to stay the night. We had more children in our family than my friends had. I shared a tiny bedroom with two sisters and there was no room to even put someone on the floor.

I do not remember ever being made to feel ashamed of our situation. I did not know such a feeling existed until the day a young girl at my school mentioned that I was wearing one of her old dresses. I thought the girl was mistaken. I had just gotten this dress from my closet. My mother had been cleaning closets and reorganized our clothes as she often did and she must have placed this new dress in the closet.

The girl did not relent. Again, she told me the dress was her old dress and that her mother had just given much of her old clothing to the church for the poor ... and that was definitely her dress.

I defended my obvious vanity by saying, "We are not poor." In my mind, we were not poor and this response validated my belief that it most certainly was not her dress, old or otherwise.

When I returned home from school that day, I was curious about the dress and asked my mother about it.

"Why do you ask?" my mother said.

She made most of our clothing and I didn't recall her making this dress. The girl's statement disturbed me because I thought it might be true and I wanted to rid myself of any shame associated with poverty. The only way to do that was to not wear the dress. But I really, really liked it. Once I relayed the story to my mother, she recognized what was at risk. She was very careful not to lie to reveal an embarrassing truth. She gave me a way to not lose face.

"Perhaps," she said, "it is a very close duplication of the one the little girl gave away. Hers must have been very similar to yours."

Now I could wear the dress that I loved with dignity.

I later found out that we did get much of our clothing from the generous parishioners at our local parish. I wish I could return to that situation to thank that young girl for the truth from which I benefited. It is not every day that we get the opportunity to thank our benefactors. But I am not so foolish as to think that if I did return to that moment I would have the courage to rise above my shame and pride. I am very grateful for God's tender ways and my mother's grace-filled wisdom.

Thus far, my stories have centered on my youth. I think it is because in our youth, our hearts are open. As we approach adulthood, grace is harder to see because we cover ourselves with more layers, more intricate disguises and an array of armor. Sometimes we behave irresponsibly in our adolescence and young adulthood. Although I was immature, I still tried to attend Mass on Sunday. I know now it was because I was drawn to the Eucharist and my heart was being strengthened.

However, there was a battle going on inside me between who I was and who I wanted to be. I didn't like the constant disagreements I was having with myself. My life choices seemed to reflect the same duality … who I was and who I desired to be. I was anguished by the conflict and wanted to live a life free from turmoil. I wanted to be who I was meant to be.

At the age of twenty, I was still living a façade in one form or another. I even entertained the thought of becoming a nun and went on a month-long retreat to the Sisters of Saint Joseph. That was a clear disaster. I knew this was not the order or the life for me. It turned out I was correct about both. There was nothing wrong with the order. I was wrong for the order and the religious life. These were all encounters with God, tenderly whispering to my heart.

Not long afterwards, I met Mike, who was a pilot and skydiver. I began going with Mike on flights and watching him skydive. Before I knew it, I was no longer content just watching him skydive, I started training to jump. It was thrilling. I loved it.

Skydiving became a new way of life for me and I stopped attending Mass. I drifted farther and farther away from my faith. With this new life, doubts and frustrations arose. I had a nagging suspicion that there was more to life than just work, friends and fun. Something was missing.

Since Mike was older than me, he wanted the relationship to move along faster and towards marriage. I considered it and accepted his proposal, thinking the commitment to marriage would eradicate this constant void. To my great disappointment, it did little or nothing to replace the deep, dull pain inside my soul. In time, I told him I was not yet ready to make the commitment to marriage. He accepted my postponement and agreed to wait for a later date.

The following weekend we went to the drop zone as usual. The only difference was Mike used another kind of parachute in addition to his usual parachute. He waited to use this parachute for the last jump of the day. That decision turned out to be fatal. On his last jump, Mike's main parachute and his reserve both malfunctioned and he plunged to his death. I watched as he got closer and closer to the ground. I began screaming, "Pull! Pull!" I saw him trying to hit the parachute to make it open, but it was no use. I was in shock. I had never witnessed such horror in all my life.

I was forced into a change that rocked my world. Change, whether I wanted it or not, was thrust upon me. I don't mean to imply that God did all this in order to get my attention and drag me kicking and screaming back to my faith. I was forced to change. And change I did.

My life spiraled out of control. I fell into a deep depression. I tried to isolate myself. I only wanted to stop for a while to think. My head was in constant turmoil, my thoughts full of confusion and guilt. If only I could think straight, I was certain I could sort through all the noise. It was only a matter of time before I would self-destruct.

At twenty, the accident was almost too much to handle. Thankfully, my mother and father were instrumental in helping restore my physical, mental and spiritual health. My skydiver friends shuttled me through the worst part of the tragedy. He was their friend, too, and they were suffering along with me. They were my closest companions during the crucial months that followed. They never left me alone. For this, I am eternally grateful. Without their vigilance, I would have fallen into despair. They were, and still are, true friends. Their faithful presence was a sign of God's grace. We drew on each other's strengths, friendships and company. He never fails to make his everlasting love known to us all.

I grew up very quickly and came face to face with reality. I was forced into reality's ugliness, its pain and the darkness of death. There is nothing more real than death and, if death is real, then so, too, is life. I could live it or I could fight it. I could accept it or reject it. I could open up the doors of life and embrace all that comes with it or I could bar the doors closed like the apostles did after the first Easter Sunday, afraid to live life. It was in this moment that our Lord opened up the doors to my heart and filled me with his tender grace. Once Christ entered the room where the apostles were, afraid for their lives, he breathed on them and gave them the Holy Spirit and his peace. He did the same for me. In his mercy and love he breathed new life in me – his life.

When we allow God to enter our lives and take hold of us, it doesn't mean that suddenly everything is perfect and you are free from troubles or challenges. To the contrary, life is full of choices and the journey to become familiar with his ways and adhere to them becomes a quest. Our hearts search and reach out to find the road that will bring us closer to him. We will continue to make mistakes and stumble along the way. It is part of our journey to cultivate a relationship with Christ and become familiar with his voice. It is how we are able to see the hand of God when grace is present in the small as well as the big miracles of everyday ordinary life.

Moments of Grace

In our youth our hearts are open. As we age grace is harder to see because we cover ourselves with more layers, more intricate disguises and an array of armor.

Sometimes it is the sufferings of life that closes our hearts and we try to protect ourselves for fear of more pain.

The moment of grace is when our Lord opens the door to your heart and fills it with his tender grace.

Do you recall a time of innocence as a child?

Are you able to trust that God will carry you through all the trials that will come into your life even though the pain may be too much to bear?

Prayer

Please Lord, open my heart that I may trust as simply as a child. Let me give you my worries, heartaches and fears. You will carry me. I desire an innocence and purity of heart.

CHAPTER 9

MERCY UPON MERCY

When we allow God to enter our lives and take hold of us, it doesn't mean that suddenly everything is perfect and you are free from troubles or challenges. To the contrary, life is full of choices and the journey to become familiar with his ways and adhere to them becomes a quest. Our hearts search and reach out to find the road that will bring us closer to him. We will continue to make mistakes and stumble along the way. God has given us a companion for our journey, his son Jesus Christ. It is part of our journey to cultivate a relationship with Christ and become familiar with his voice. It is how we are able to see the hand of God when grace is present in the small as well as the big miracles of everyday, ordinary life.

Sometimes the perceived absence of his presence calls attention to the most glorious mysteries. Thinking all was lost with my younger brother, God intervened with a miracle in my own life.

My brother grew up with many difficult challenges. At a young age, he became an alcoholic. He got into trouble with the law which led to jail time. He descended into a vicious cycle of tragedy and prison. My entire family was constantly dealing with heartbreak. Just when we thought he had learned a lesson, or figured out his latest calamity, he would plunge into yet another.

Many in the family had given up hope that he would ever change his ways. My mother and father were his sole supporters and, although we all continued to pray for him, we did little in the way of assistance. My mother and father continued to visit him in prison. They sent him the necessary clothing, little amounts of money and wrote to him often. They prayed continuously for him and begged many priest friends to help counsel him. They took him back into their home when he was released ... only to go through it all over again a few months later.

My brother was in prison when my mother passed away. A friend of my father arranged for my brother to say goodbye to my mother at the wake. He arrived in a bright orange jumpsuit, chains and police escorts. He was neither allowed to talk to his family nor touch any of us. We had to stand at a distance and watch his sorrow on display.

It was humiliating and heartbreaking to see. I was angry that he had to shame our mother, even in her death. How disgraceful, I thought. Wasn't it bad enough to shame her when she was alive, but must he do so at her death as well? Eventually, I saw the pain on his face and I relented. I recognized the sorrow in my brother's eyes. I witnessed his humility in arriving under those horrible circumstances and the gratitude for being allowed to see mom one last time. We all shouted our love from a distance. We pleaded with him to change and to come back a new man.

But this was not to be. He continued down the same destructive path and even worse. Finally, my father sent him to a program in Florida, in hopes of helping him turn his life around. Unfortunately, he walked out of the community and never went back.

For several years we did not know if he was dead or alive until one day he called. Often, he would call someone in the family and would manage a few sentences before it became apparent that he was intoxicated. At least we knew he was alive. We all continued to pray. I went from great reservations to outright disbelief. Where was God in all this destruction? Why hadn't God answered our prayers? My mother and father had prayed their entire lives for my brother to no avail. I didn't believe prayer was the answer any longer, nor was God ever going to change my brother. God seemed absent in this situation and I no longer believed he would or could help.

Then one day, out of the blue, my phone rang. It was my brother. After talking for several minutes, I did not detect a hint of alcohol or drugs. But I had been here before, so I was cautious. I began to talk about my two young daughters and told him how much joy they had brought to our family. He was silent. After a few minutes, I asked him if he was all right. He paused for a second and softly responded, "I did not know you had two more children."

This made me sit up and listen more carefully. He said this with such regret and sorrow. He told me his life had changed. Honestly, I didn't believe him. I had heard it all before. I responded with the same doubt in my voice and told him to live one day at a time. I wished him well, told him I would continue to pray for him and hung up, expecting to hear from him within a few days in his usual drunken stupor.

I called the rest of the family to tell them my brother was still alive. They, too, had heard from him. We all expressed our doubts but we were hopeful. A month later, he called again. Again he was sober. He called to apologize for causing so much heartache and asked for forgiveness. I forgave him in a backhanded way.

"Yes," I said bitterly, "you can have my forgiveness if you actually stay sober and clean."

He understood my reservations because he had expressed his own uncertainty. "One day at a time," he said.

I just didn't believe it would last. I knew as soon as I put down my defenses and believed him, I would be disappointed to find him right back in the gutter again. It was just too risky and too painful to watch him self-destruct. I did not want to become vulnerable to those raw emotions again. I saw my parents go through too much as he drew the life out of them.

As time went on, I was waiting for the other shoe to drop. I found myself thinking of him often and offering up a prayer or two, while doubting it would actually be heard. I realized I had hope. Real hope. I tried to tamp it down and convince myself it would be no different than before.

I discussed this with my father and other family members. We were all in agreement and felt equally apprehensive. Yet, deep down inside, we stayed hopeful. We loved my bother but were afraid to let him back into our hearts.

Finally, my father displayed the love of our heavenly Father. He reached out to his son. "There is nothing you can do that will stop me from loving you," he insisted.

My father had the most to lose. It was my father's love and my father's actions that my brother had rejected. However, it was my father's display of God's merciful love towards my brother that opened up the hearts of the rest of us. He would let nothing come between his son and himself. He forgave his son and labored to tether their relationship and their love for good. He extended his hand to welcome him home. It had been six long years since he had seen him. He wanted to rebuild their relationship. He wanted to embrace him, to love him completely, as he was never allowed to before. He had been lost but now was found. It was the prodigal son happening right before our very eyes.

My brother never turned back. His life is a genuine miracle. He had discovered the depths of God's gentle mercy and I am a witness to this beautiful mystery. It is a testament to anyone who wishes to see the power of God's love. It taught me that there is mercy and forgiveness beyond my control. God's mercy was working on my brother without our family knowing it. To us he could have been dead but his brother Jesus was pulling him out of the pig pits. When we became vulnerable and opened ourselves to the Christ within him, we experienced Christ in all his glory. We were forced to set aside our stipulations, obstacles and preconceived notions we had about him and see what Christ wanted us to see. Jesus revealed himself to us in all his beauty and splendor and in the process exposed us to our own humanity. It is his goodness and mercy on display.

There is a little of the prodigal son's brother in all of us. The older son told his father, "Look, all these years I served you and not once did I disobey your orders; yet you never gave me even a young goat to feast on with my friends." (Luke 15:29) Just as my father encouraged us to welcome his son back, the father of the prodigal son replied, "My son, you are here with me always; everything I have is yours. But now we must celebrate and rejoice, because your brother was dead and has come to life again; he was lost and has been found." (Luke 15:24) It took a while for my father's joy to be my joy. I needed my father's mercy to touch me as well as my brother.

Notice the father's response to the older son is the same as the response to the returning son. Just as the father extends mercy to his prodigal son, he reminds his eldest that his merciful love continues to be ever present and never failing for both of them. The father loves him for who he is and has always loved him. Not for what he has done. Just as God loves us for who we are and not for what we do. We must recognize that we need our Father's love and will freely return love with no strings attached. The father in the story is celebrating the fact that the younger son has discovered life is better with his father. The prodigal son humbles himself, willing to do any menial task just to be in his presence. Penniless, starving and almost unrecognizable in filth, he is embraced.

When the prodigal son left with money in hand, he thought he had all he needed to be happy in the world. He didn't think of his father until he was fighting the pigs for food. How low did my brother go before climbing out of the pits? How far do we go before we realize things are better in our Father's house?

In my first chapter, I shared how I became the prodigal daughter wandering away from the heavenly Father's care. I pursued what I thought would make me happy. Then it literally all came crashing down when my fiancé fell to his death. Unlike the prodigal son's brother, I had Jesus, our forgiving brother. Carried by his grace, he found me, washed me and put on a clean garment of his mercy.

When Jesus brings us home, our Father sees us returning from a distance, he races to greet us and immediately, without questions, orders the finest robes and jewelry to be given to us. He treats us as royalty. We are brothers and sisters of the king.

The story of the prodigal son tells us how our heavenly Father loves us and how we are to love him and one another in return. He loves unconditionally. Do I love God without conditions? Do I have expectations of God that involve him solving my problems? Do I have an expectation that God must do something to change my pain or unpleasant circumstances? If I am honest, I don't always embrace my pain or cross. I beg for God's help but not always without preconditions of how our Lord can manage the problem. Worse yet, I tell him how to resolve my predicament, as though I know what is best.

I once heard a priest ask, "Am I willing to go to greater lengths and endure a little more pain in order to get something that I like or love?" The answer is yes. We all will, won't we? And, if I am willing to go to greater lengths to do something that may involve being uncomfortable, is it not worth the effort? Isn't that why I am willing to endure a bit more pain? But if there is no pain or effort in acquiring this desired tangible, is it worth having? This is where the older brother is stuck. He is uncomfortable and resentful. Many of us are uncomfortable with others receiving attention that we think we deserve. With God our works don't earn his love just as the elder son's dutiful works didn't earn his father's love. Our Father just loves. We don't deserve our Father's love. We are gifted. Any pain we have is our gift back to him.

I would say many of us, myself included, cannot readily see goodness when we are hurting and react the same as the older brother. Our preconceived notions of how God should love us is not as God loves. Recognition of our weaknesses makes us more human and the more human we are, the closer we get to the Father. We recognize our need for him. By always keeping this need in front of us, we humbly beg for and accept the Father's love. It keeps our relationship dependent upon the good ... even if that good is painful.

Whether we are the prodigal son or the elder brother, Jesus embraces us. He washes us, feeds us, and rejoices that we are together in our Father's house. He gives us a clean robe and a crown.

For the prodigal son, he was probably bathed by servants. I'm sure the elder son did not wash off the pig grime. We have Jesus, our brother, washing us. Like Peter, we might initially refuse to allow Christ to do such a mortifying task. Peter thought that Jesus was stooping to a level that was unnecessary and unfit for the Son of Man to be doing for him. He also wanted to prevent Jesus from seeing his true sinfulness. Peter did not understand until Jesus said, "Unless I wash you, you will have no inheritance with me." (John 13:8) Then Peter responded with full understanding, "Master, then not only my feet, but my hands and head as well." (John 13:9) He recognized immediately that he must permit Jesus to love all of him, including his most disproportionate self.

We all must succumb to this humiliating task of letting Christ love even our most repulsive and despicable warts. It is not something we can do ourselves. This is where the elder son in the prodigal son parable refuses to accept the invitation to celebrate the younger brother's return from a corrupt life and to participate fully in the joy of his father's love. He doesn't accept the invitation to be completely loved by his father. The returning son embraces this love and so does Peter. The prodigal son's inheritance is restored through the mercy of his father and Peter gains his inheritance accepting Jesus' love and mercy.

What about my inheritance? The washing of Peter's feet and the prodigal son remind me to keep my wounds in front of me so that my need for Christ is always visible … and I remember to beg Christ to love me entirely, warts and all. If I refuse his love, I refuse his invitation to participate in the relationship that I was so clearly made for.

Just like Peter and the prodigal son participated in a feast, we are called to the banquet of the Eucharist. It is our perfect invitation to come and receive his love; no strings attached. Both the prodigal son and the washing of the feet were invitations to the relationship with the Father's love and the Eucharist is the completion of the relationship. He even says, "Whoever eats my flesh and drinks my blood remains in me and I in him." (John 6:56)

Like the returning son, I freely want the love of the Father. Once I have discovered the love of the Father and have experienced his tender mercy despite all my warts and ugliness, I want to reciprocate freely. Jesus tells me how.

He commands us to love one another. We are made for love. To love one another is to love him. The more we love, the greater his love. The sacraments bring us to foot of the cross and fuse our hearts to his love. With the Eucharist it is the purest and most authentic of his love … the gift of himself to be with us always.

Mercy upon mercy. My brother received mercy. I received mercy. How do I give thanks? How do I show my love? How am I to love one another as Christ? As he feeds me, he challenges me and tests me, asking, "Do you love me?"

In my journey, I've stumbled along, tripping and falling, but got back up, carried by his merciful grace. He continued to pull me through doubt, desperation and even despair. When I asked myself, "Do I believe? Do I really believe?" The answer always came back the same, "Yes, I believe."

When I found myself with real hope, my faith in Christ changed my life and the lives of others. Hope that despite the circumstances, Jesus was and is always there to bring his life, his mercy and his love to me. These three gifts are the core to our journey through life: faith, hope and love "but the greatest of these is love." (I Corinthians 13:13)

Once I surrendered my life to Christ, my life focus began to shift. Christ became my longing as I looked for him in my relationships, my surroundings and my heart. I fixed my eyes on him to find him wherever I could. It is not enough to sit back and let life pass by. It took work to adhere to Christ and become aware of his presence.

To advance boldly towards him and establish a familial relationship, I had to recognize his voice, his ways and he himself. As I listened to his voice, he moved my heart to compassion. Listening for his voice meant listening everywhere. You never know when a message will touch your heart.

I was attending a Bible study class at St. Agnes Parish while my girls were at school. Guest speakers came to give a testimony of their journey in the faith or some particular witness to that week's topic of bible study. Barbara Kirby, the Director of the St. Agnes Day Room, discussed her own personal journey in the Catholic faith and the founding of the Day Room. Barbara spoke with such eloquence and beauty about feeding people who are poor and loving the unloved and accepting the rejected. I was overcome with a desire to know and love them as well.

She spoke directly from her heart. Christ began moving my heart toward something greater. Initially, I was uncomfortable interacting with people who are poor, homeless and mentally ill. Yet here was this woman talking about listening to them, loving them and embracing them completely, just as Christ had done.

She did not withhold love from anyone because she said, "It is not my love to give. Who am I to discriminate in handing out God's love when it is he who sends the needy to me? Everyone who comes to the Day Room is entitled to experience God's lavish love."

I was struck by her authenticity and generosity. I wanted what she had. It was real because she was real. So when she invited anyone to come and see what the Day Room was all about, I jumped at the chance.

My first experience was working in the "back," folding and sorting donated clothes. It reminded me of what it must have been like when my own mother came looking for clothing, especially pretty dresses, for her children. I had come full circle, helping to do the same for those who were in need. I didn't mind doing this, but I was unable to see God's grace without interacting with the people who were seeking help. How was I going to observe this lovely lady in action and learn to love and give love as she did?

I took it upon myself to go into the main area of the Day Room one day after Mass. I just happened to come in when an older gentleman was making toast but had to leave to do something else. He never hesitated, just handing me the butter knife and telling me to toast as much as I could to fill the tray. "They serve at 9 a.m. after prayer," he said.

I stayed and toasted from that day on, watching Barbara and all the others who had a special brand of love for Christ, whose hearts were moved like mine to serve Him. I am grateful beyond words that God led me to this place to find him still alive and well, living in our midst. What Christ can do when we open ourselves to his merciful love is more than I ever expected. I know it is not possible to be perfect but, through Christ, we are perfected.

In serving those in need, I have come to learn that eliminating or solving poverty is not necessarily the objective. Rather, it is a privilege to love the person we serve, the way Christ loves. We don't have to be somebody or do something in order for God to love us. It is in the everyday, ordinary circumstances of just being together that he is drawn to us and us to him. In loving those in need, we share ourselves with them and they share their love with us. I have never felt more loved than by the beautiful people of the Day Room. They love me just the way I am with no strings attached and I love them back. It is the purest kind of love and I am privileged to experience it.

However, many encounters at the Day Room did not always lead to the outcomes I expected. On one such occasion, it was through one person's weaknesses that I was able to see my own. I had the privilege of meeting myself.

A young mother was facing a difficult situation and had to make some hard, life-changing decisions. In advising her on how to reach the desired outcome, I got a glimpse of myself. It is not always a pleasant experience until you accept the view as a gift from God and allow his merciful grace to wash over you. Mercy, upon Mercy, upon Mercy. It was with this exercise that I was able to recognize that we are all the same. We are all human and we all seek the same thing—to love and be loved. It is what speaks to every human heart. It is what we are made for.

Becoming comfortable around people who are poor, homeless or mentally ill was not easy for me. It meant opening myself up to my own humanity. It meant putting myself at the disposal of God's will to answer his call. It also meant placing myself in the uncomfortable position of having to make a judgment, a judgment based on experience that comes from within my heart and to know the voice I must follow.

I come to the Day Room for the same reasons and with the same needs as everyone else. I desire to be accepted despite my weaknesses, my sins and my imperfections. I come to be loved by someone. That someone is Christ. It is here that the love of Christ is given because it is where the body of Christ (the Church) in the Word made Flesh lives. My heart's desires are discovered when I find Jesus alive in those needing unconditional love. I have come to know his voice in people I encounter in everyday circumstances. He reveals his abounding love through my co-workers, my children, my neighbors, my husband and perfect strangers. And it is the Day Room that has given me the opportunity to familiarize myself with his presence and his voice.

His grace is truly everywhere because he is everywhere. He is the ever-present goodness that I witness, experience and encounter in my own life and in all the lives around me. It is through this beautiful encounter that I can participate in bringing Christ's love to others.

God's personal love for the five of us has seized us in our quest of writing this book. We have allowed ourselves to be led by him. He yearns to be present to us here and now. He makes himself known and accessible through his Spirit by means of scripture and the sacraments and, above all, through the movement of our hearts through the Church. In writing this book, we have searched for his will through all of these means, in order to bring the life of grace to all who crave his presence, his love and his touch.

Our beloved Pope Francis speaks eloquently about God's desire to be with us. God will go to great lengths to invite us into his life and meet us where we are. The Pope encourages all of us to meet our brothers and sisters where they are in their life. It is our call as Christians.

Barbara Arbuckle's image of a tapestry has drawn us all together. Grace is woven throughout all of our lives, from the smallest to the grandest of designs. Jesus is our golden thread. He will always be there, whispering in the small ways, hoping to get your attention.

Meet God where you are today. Allow him to lavishly shower upon you his loving grace and mercy. He is alive and well today, tomorrow and forever. He has already invited us into his life. It is your turn. All you need to do is to give over the threads of your life to weave them into his master plan.

Moments of Grace

Ask for Jesus' mercy. Look into all the corners of your life that need the touch of Jesus' love and mercy.

Accept his mercy. Spend time in silence to listen to how he wants to bless you. Be open to the little ways Jesus is reaching out his love to you.

Share his mercy. Look to those around you to be the hands and heart of Christ.

Prayer

Open my eyes Lord that I might see your face.
Open my ears that I might hear your voice.
Open my heart that it be filled with your love.
Open my mind that it be filled with thankfulness and praise.

EPILOGUE

Grace is freely given to all from God. If you allow it, grace will change you. God knows us intimately and knows what graces we need.

God's greatest gift to us is Jesus. Allow Jesus to love you and experience your own personal love story with him. Jesus will carry you through any darkness and be your strength.

May you be filled with joy in knowing you are a precious child of God. His love for you is beyond measure. And may you find comfort and hope in knowing that whatever comes your way, you will be carried by grace.

Grace is alive and well as Jesus promised St. Faustina:

"When a soul approaches Me with trust, I fill it with such an abundance of graces that it cannot contain them within itself, but radiates them to other souls." (1074)

REFERENCES

Unless otherwise noted, scripture passages have been taken from: New American Bible. 2010. Washington, DC: Confraternity of Christian Doctrine.

Arbuckle, B. (2009). *Life Lessons from the Little Ones.* West Conshohocken, PA: Infinity Publishing

Arrupe, P. Retrieved from https://iamadoctorofchrist.wordpress. com/2012/06/03/arrupe-prayer-cards-available-at-the-oratory/

Bracken, J. *You Gave Me Peace of Mind.* [Recorded by The Spaniels]. On *The Very Best of the Spaniels.* VeeJay Records. (1956).

Divine Mercy Chaplet. Retrieved from http://thedivinemercy.org/ message/.

Hayes, G. *Angel Rays.* [Recorded by Sissel]. On *My Heart.* Decca. (2004).

In Ian's Boots. Retrieved from http://www.iniansboots.org/home. html.

Kairos Prison Ministry International, Inc. Retrieved from http:// kpmifoundation.org/index.php.

Kowalska, M. F. (2008). *Diary of Maria Faustina Kowalska: Divine Mercy in My Soul.* Stockbridge: Marion Press.

McGrane, J. (2006). *Saints to Lean On: Spiritual Companions for Illness.* Cincinnati: St. Anthony Messenger Press.

McGrane, J. (2011). *Saints for Healing: Stories of Courage and Hope.* Cincinnati: St. Anthony Messenger Press.

Missionary Sisters of the Sacred Heart of Jesus. Retrieved from mscreading.org.

O'Connor, *Flannery O'Connor Quotes.* Retrieved from http://www.goodreads.com/author/quotes/22694.Flannery O'Connor.

St. Therese of Lisieux. 1897. *The Yellow Notebook.* Retrieved from Archives Du Carmel De Lisieux http://www.archives-carmel-lisieux.fr/english/carmel/index.php/carnet-jaune/2120-carnet-jaune-juin.

Taylor Berry, E. (2002). *Then, I Look At The Cross.* (Unpublished manuscript).

Wright, W. (2005). *Caryll Houselander: Essential Writings (Modern Spiritual Masters).* Maryknoll, NY: Orbis Books.

ABOUT THE AUTHORS

*B*arbara Arbuckle is a retired Catholic School Kindergarten Teacher. She earned her bachelor's degree in Elementary Education from West Chester University. Barbara self-published a book entitled Life Lessons from the Little Ones. It is the words, wit and wisdom of the children. The children remind us of God's great love for us.

She continues to write about her love for the Lord. In addition to participation in her parish's charismatic prayer group, she considers reading scripture, prayer and the rosary very important in her life. After retiring she cared for her mother for seven years. She now enjoys time with her husband, son, daughter, son-in-law and three grandsons. Barbara lives with her husband of over forty years in West Chester, Pennsylvania.

Elisa Taylor Berry, BS, has taught at the primary, elementary and middle school levels. She earned her bachelor's degree in Early Childhood Education/Elementary Education from Chestnut Hill College.

Since leaving the teaching profession in 2005, she has been involved in many parish outreach ministries. The primary ministries in which she has concentrated most of her efforts have been evangelization of the faith through her writing, prayer outside abortion clinics, making and distributing World Mission Rosaries and volunteering with the Kairos Prison Ministry.

She has been a lay associate of the Missionary Sisters of the Sacred Heart since June, 2000. As a lay missionary of the Sacred Heart she is "called to be the heart of God on earth." Elisa and her husband reside in Oreland, Pennsylvania, near their two children and eight grandchildren. Her latest evangelization endeavor is her website, heavenhelpus.net. This website offers a place where one can explore the many ways heaven is trying to help us!

Arlene C. Finocchiaro, MS, is a retired occupational therapist with more than thirty years of experience working with special-needs children. Since retirement she has focused on writing to share life experiences graced by God's love and write stories for children who so enriched her professional career.

Arlene is involved in parish activities and is an associate of the Sisters of Saint Joseph. For eight years, she participated in the Wilmington diocesan healing ministry.

She lives in Wilmington, Delaware, with her husband, a retired sports journalist. She earned her bachelor's degree in occupational therapy from Mount Mary College in Milwaukee and an advanced master's degree in occupational therapy from Towson State University. Her education was furthered with a certificate in severe disabilities from the University of Delaware.

She is a member of the Society of Children's Book Writers and Illustrators and the Catholic Writers Guild.

Janice McGrane, SSJ, MA, is a Sister of Saint Joseph from Chestnut Hill, Philadelphia. She is a spiritual director, disability activist, environmental advocate, and board chairperson for Liberty Resources, Inc., a Center for Independent Living.

One of her primary interests is the spirituality of disability. She received her master's degree in spirituality from Chestnut Hill College and her bachelor's degree in English from Penn State University.

Her books on the saints—*Saints to Lean On: Spiritual Companions for Illness and Disability* and *Saints for Healing: Stories of Courage and Hope*— share how saints faced their afflictions and were sources of healing.

Annette Hug is the fifth of seven children. She is a voracious reader and has always loved writing. After getting married, she attended several community colleges while starting a family and moving around the country. Annette found her love for working with God's chosen poor at the St. Agnes Day Room in West Chester, PA. She continues to reside with her husband and children in West Chester, PA.